TPOI
KASANDRA

The Problem of Islam – Kasandra

All Rights Reserved. No reproduction, copy or transmission of the publication may be made without written permission. No paragraph or section of this publication may be reproduced copied or transmitted save with written permission or in accordance with the provisions of the Copyright Act 1956 (as amended). Copyright 2024 of the author. The right of the 'Kasandra' to be identified as the author of this work has been asserted in accordance with the Copyright Designs and Patents Act 1988. A copy of this book is deposited with the British Library.

ISBN: 9798343985009

#TPOI

(REV250113)

First published October 2024

Index

1, Disclaimer — 4
2, Preamble — 5
3, The Real Far-Right — 6
4, My Position — 7
5, Economics — 8
6, War — 11
7, Kindi's Dilemma — 15
8, Hume — 22
9, Schopenhauer — 23
10, Nietzsche — 24
11, Allah Does Not Exist — 25
12, When is a Religion Not a Religion? — 38
13, Character of Muhammad — 41
14, Character of Islam — 42
15, General Demographics — 47
16, Separation of Powers (Locke) — 48
17, Failure Export Cycle — 49
18, Submission = Good? — 50
19, Strongmen — 51
20, Denial — 52
21, Imposters — 55
22, Lack of Criticism — 56
23, Beliefs Fail — 57
24, How Islam Advances — 59
25, Loonies — 60
26, War on Empiricism — 61
27, Concealment — 62
28, Egypt — 63
29, Freedom of Religion — 69
30, Sectarianism — 70
31, Mercantilism — 71
32, Pre-emptive Retaliation — 72
33, Quibble All You Like — 75
34, Catch 22 — 76
35, Immigrants Saved My Life — 77
36, The Right Want Immigration — 78
37, The Religion is the Problem — 79
38, What Would I do if I Were a Bad Person? — 80
39, To Do — 81
40, Thought Experiment — 82
41, Grounds For Optimism — 83
42, Conclusion — 85

1 – Disclaimer

I wish every Muslim in the world, peace, happiness, prosperity, good health and a long life. It is not ok to hate Muslims. They are human beings, equals, and should be treated with courtesy. I have worked with Muslims for years and could not ask for more decent, pleasant, upstanding colleagues. When teaching, I was always careful to give time, help and marks fairly. There was never a single cross word, I was never rude, I'm proud of the help I gave and grateful for the help I received. So, if you've picked up this book hoping to find justification for unpleasantness, please look elsewhere.

For the purposes of this book, I am drawing a distinction between people and ideas, I don't hate anyone, I disagree with bad ideas. To clarify:

Attacking ideas = OK
Attacking people = Not OK

Those who disagree will do the opposite. I will look for general patterns rather than draw conclusions from specific examples. Again, those who disagree will do the opposite.

2 – Preamble

The front cover of this book has two words 'TPOI' (The Problem of Islam) and 'Kasandra' (my pen name). The former is to protect my readers, the latter to protect myself. The fact that I have had to do this demonstrates there is a problem. I am publishing this book for the minimum amount to cover printing costs and writing anonymously so I can't be accused of courting notoriety. I have done this to pre-emptively diffuse any accusation that I am writing out of self-interest - I am writing out of the general interest.

The title comes from Alcoholics Anonymous: *'The first step is admitting there is a problem'*.

To keep things brisk I will mention things in passing (Locke/Hume/Kant etc) with the briefest possible outline, even though they warrant whole books to themselves.

3 – The Real 'Far-Right'

Islam means 'submission'. It is homophobic, creationist, patriarchal, mercantilist, supremacist, mono-cultural, territorial, expansionist, censorious, authoritarian, anti-democratic, socially conservative, coercive and segregated. No Islamic state in history has advocated free speech, minority rights, artistic expression, social mobility, women's rights, gay rights or any of the other touchstone issues of the Left. Islam is an extreme right-wing ideology by every conceivable measure. Additionally, it should be noted that within Islam cruelty to animals isn't just permitted – it's prescribed.

In contemporary society anyone opposed to Islam is thoughtlessly dismissed as 'far-right' but that is just a mantra people use to exempt themselves from careful thought. If we attribute nouns and adjectives on the basis of evidence, it is clear that Islam makes societies more right-wing not less. Every argument against this book will be a genuinely right-wing fanatic seeking to make more territory more Islamic.

4 – My Position

My outlook is conventional to the point of tedium. I am a social democrat, atheist, vegetarian, environmentalist. I am against racism, support gay rights, human rights, peace, free speech, and feminism. Yet somehow I find myself in opposition to the rest of society. What makes me different to the pretend radicals is that I apply these values consistently and do not admit exceptions where it is fashionable to do so. Consequently I find myself surrounded by people who claim to have a similar outlook to myself, their Kantian 'thing-in-itself' is virtue incarnate, but when we mute the soundtrack and watch the movie we see them advancing an ideology that is the antithesis of what they advocate. The kindest thing I can say about them is they are guilty of intellectual dishonesty, it's time to call out tyranny masquerading as ethics.

5 – Islamic Economics

There are three types of Islamic economy:
1 - Commodity economies.
2 - Tourism economies.
3 - Collapsed economies.

The commodity economies are countries like Saudi Arabia and Kuwait. They export oil for money - without oil they would be collapsed economies. Commodity economies are neo-capitalist and environmentally catastrophic. They sell fuel to be burned and their buildings and cities are energy intensive.

The tourism economies are countries like Egypt, Turkey or the Maldives. They don't have commodities to export, so they stave off economic collapse through tourism. Again they are neo-capitalist - if you walk down the street you will be hassled for money. Again they are environmentally catastrophic. Settled, indigenous cultures tend to be more intimately integrated with their local environment, they consume less, repair more and recycle more than communities less integrated to their locality. Tourism destroys the indigenous cultures of both visitors and visited - and of course there is the pollution of the journey.

The collapsed economies are countries like Afghanistan or Pakistan. Their minerals are not in demand, people don't want to go there on holiday, so they collapse.

The commodity and tourism-based economies have something obvious in common – they monetise territory. Commodity economies sell their minerals and tourism economies effectively grant short term leases to their country - so they're like a hotel but on a much bigger scale. But basically, with commodity and tourism economies there is a direct corelation between money and territory. So there is no alternative Islamic economic model and certainly no left-wing Islamic economic model. Commodity economies transport things to people, tourism economies transport people to and from things, and collapsed economies make no money. Indeed, it's worth noting that if we exclude the collapsed economies (on the grounds that they aren't actually economies at all) we could say that all Islamic *economies* are neo-capitalist.

Now think about how you and your colleagues earn money to pay your bills. Maybe you are a teacher, a graphic designer, tattoo artist, hairdresser, structural engineer, whatever. In non-Islamic economies people monetise their minds to earn money - we have skills and knowledge which we sell. The more knowledge and skills we accumulate, the more we can earn. Islam assumes that the ultimate document was written 1500 years ago so any new ideas published in the meantime are not only trivial but immoral. Intellectual endeavour is actively prohibited in Islam. Well, if you learn less, you are going to earn less - the lack of creativity and prosperity in Islamic states is corelation, not coincidence.

Islam has become mighty not through its virtues but our vices - polluting idiots in the West pay for it to be mighty. As western economies switch to renewable energy, commodity economies that cannot become tourism economies will become collapsed economies, so the only way Islam can survive economically is to:

1, Present cities like Dubai as tax heavens to attract super-rich tax-dodgers.
2, Dupe useful idiots in the West to give them aid.
3, Invade thought-based economies and exploit our rights/welfare systems to incubate Islam's dysfunctional ideology.

One option not open to Islam is to adopt an intelligence-based economy, because to do that is to be un-Islamic.

Note: The 'Labour Theory of Value' (originated by Smith and Ricardo, then later taken up by Marx) proposes that the value of something is determined by the labour required to produce it. This idea was the prime generator of the machine age of modernism that flourished till the 1970s. However, now we are living in a Kantian world in which the mental is primary and the physical merely secondary; consequently, we have transitioned to a Mental Theory of Value (MToV). Value is now determined by the thought invested in something rather than the object itself. For example:
1, Porche cars are better built than Tesla cars, but Tesla is wiping out Porche because Porche cars are dumb whereas Tesla cars are self-driving.
2, The biggest companies in the world barely *make* anything.
3, The value of art by Warhol or Haring resides, not in the object, but the idea that generated it.
Wealth used to be about hands, rearranging minerals or moving things/people; now it's about skills, ideas and intelligence; so if you think all truth is in the Koran then enjoy staying poor.

6 - War

Here is a map of war (2024)

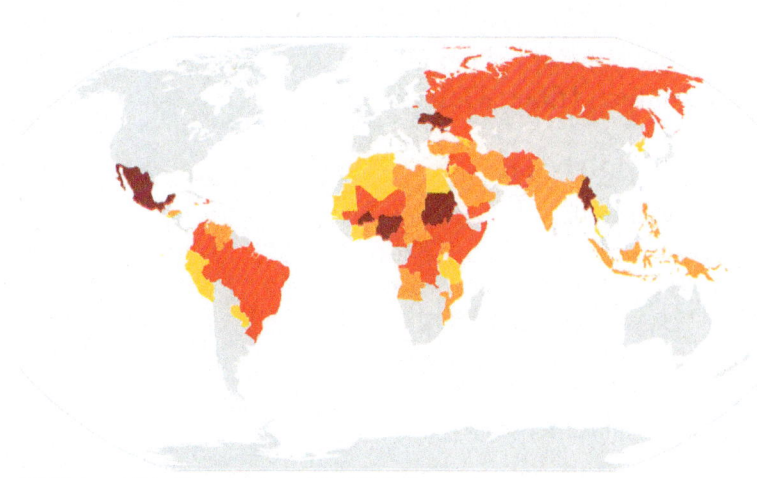

(Wikimedia Commons 09.09.24)

… and here is a map of Islam (2024)

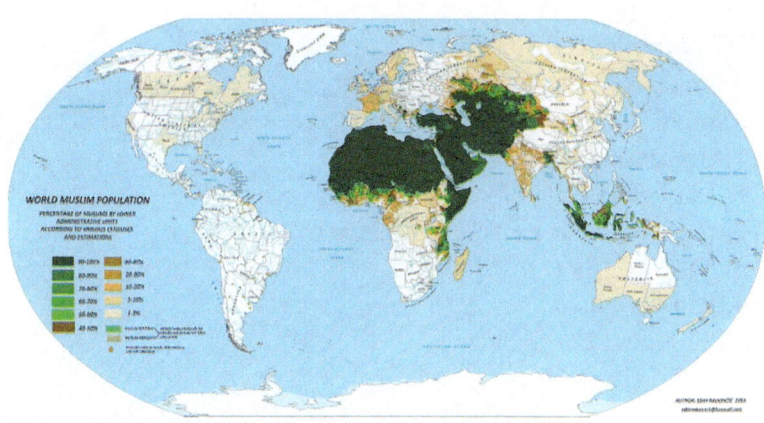

(https://www.nationsonline.org 09.09.24)

By their very nature wars are constantly in a state of flux. So by the time you read this some conflicts may have escalated, others de-escalated. But it would be foolish to deny the corelation between these two maps. (I did a similar exercise

11

10 years ago and the maps were broadly similar) Wherever there is Islam there seems to be war. If anything, these two maps under-represent the corelation between Islam and war because the large geographical masses of Russia and Brazil have a distorting affect graphically. Now let's go through the list of conflicts (from Wikipedia).

Major wars (10,000 or more combat-related deaths in current or previous year)

1, Myanmar conflict.
2, Arab/Israeli conflict.
3, Insurgency in the Maghreb.
4, Mexican drug war.
5, Russian/Ukraine war.
6, Sudanese civil war.

Wars (1,000–9,999 combat-related deaths in current or previous year)

7, Colombian conflict.
8, Afghan conflict.
9, Somali Civil War.
10, Communal conflicts in Nigeria.
11, Iraqi conflict.
12, Insurgency in Khyber Pakhtunkhwa.
13, Kivu conflict.
14, Rio favelas.
15, Sudanese conflicts.
16, Boko Harem insurgency.
17, Syrian civil war.
18, Yemeni civil war.
19, Anglophone crisis.
20, Ethiopian civil conflict.
21, Gang war Haiti.

Minor conflicts (100–999 combat-related deaths in current or previous year)

22, Kurdish separatism in Iran.
23, Kurdish/Turkish conflict.
24, Jamaican political conflict.
25, India/Pakistan conflict.
26, Insurgency in Balochistan.
27, Insurgency in Northeast India.
28, Papua conflict.
29, Naxalite Maoist insurgency.
30, Civil conflict in the Philippines.
31, Cabinda War.
32, Nagorno-Karabakh conflict.
33, Ethnic violence in Papua New Guinea.
34, Internal conflict in Bangladesh.
35, Conflict in the Niger Delta.
36, Libyan crisis.
37, Central African Republic civil war.
38, Philippine drug war.
39, Insurgency in Cabo Delgado.
40, Islamic State insurgency North Caucasus.
41, Honduran gang crackdown.

Skirmishes and clashes
(fewer than 100 combat-related deaths in current and previous year)

42, Iraqi/Kurdish conflict.
43, Korean conflict.
44, Katanga insurgency.
45, Western Sahara conflict.
46, Chittagong Hill Tracts conflict.
47, Peruvian conflict.
48, Islamic terrorism Egypt.
49, Casamance conflict.
50, Lord's Resistance Army Insurgency.

51, Georgian/Ossetian conflict.
52, South Thailand insurgency.
53, Insurgency in Paraguay.
54, Insurgency in Northern Chad.
55, Ecuadorian drug war.
56, Salvadoran gang crackdown.
57, Western DR Congo Clashes.

You will see I've written some in red, the rest in black. The conflicts written in red are the ones where one set of belligerents are seeking to make more territory more Islamic. So although only about 15% of humans are Muslim, Islam is a generator of the majority of wars - and a majority of the biggest wars! Yes there are some exceptions (like the Ukraine conflict and the Mexican drug war) but these are exceptional, and specific examples to not demonstrate general corelations (if one smoker is healthy it doesn't prove that smoking isn't unhealthy). It is not fanciful to suggest that if every Muslim became an atheist tomorrow, war would virtually end for the first time in history.

Muhammad was the leader of an army, and it's only natural that an ideology written by a soldier should be inclined towards the domination of territory. Sure enough conflicts seem to occur where the philosophy of the soldier predominates. And of course it doesn't take much imagination to see these, not as separate conflicts at all, but as separate skirmishes in a single intergenerational, international Islamic war against the rest of humanity. It is curious that people calling themselves 'internationalists' seem determined to deny that the Islamic world war even exists! Look at your own society. Where is it most war like? Where are the most stabbings? Where are women treated like a joy division? Where are gangs battling for territory? In the rural areas where there are the fewest police? No. The most war-like parts of your society are where the philosophy of the soldier predominates.

7 - Kindi's Dilemma

Al-Kindi (801-873) was a great Islamic intellectual who pioneered the translation of Aristotelian texts into Arabic. But Aristotle's god does not have human characteristics, it is a 'first cause' in a mechanistic universe. As a Muslim, Kindi was obliged to reject the idea of an eternal universe - he *had* to believe in creation. But Kindi sought to reconcile these two schools of thought. It was helpful that, at this time the great intellectual developments were taking place in the salons, rather than the mosques, but still his project was politically sensitive - at one point his library was confiscated! Kindi's great contribution was the revival of Greek philosophy and the preservation of the apparatus of philosophy itself.

Al-Farabi (872-950) asserted that the Universe is indeed eternal, which was closer to Aristotle's position than Kindi had been. This was a departure from the orthodox line. Additionally he diverged from Islamic doctrine by claiming that creation was necessary and not a gift from a benevolent God. But he was similar to Kindi in that he sustained Islam's engagement with Greek ideas and sought to use the Greek system to make sense of the Islamic faith.

Al-Biruni (973-1050) was an astonishing polymath who, almost singlehandedly, invented anthropology. How did he invent social science? With his book 'The India' which was an appreciation of Hindu culture. Previously Islamic clerics dismissed Hinduism as polytheistic idol worship. Biruni showed Hinduism to be a far more subtle and complex intellectual construction than the Islamic world had given it credit for. He described the Hindus and Greeks as 'two families in the same house'. He also wrote extensively on the timing of the religious festivals of the Buddhists, Sogdians, Zoroastrians, Christians, Jews and Pagans. His lifelong obsession with time led him to the study of the planetary motion. His proposition that planets moved in ellipses anticipated the work of Kepler. This posed a problem for the religious (and followers of Farabi) who asserted that the heavens *must* move in perfect circles rather than wobble along in ellipses (as is actually the case). It's no surprise that Biruni flourished in an environment where there was relatively little disparagement of non-Islamic science. His work was largely ignored in the Islamic world.

The most original Islamic philosopher, Avicenna (980-1037) was (justifiably) immodest. He drank a lot and actively pursued worldly sexual pleasures (for which I do not blame him). Perennially controversial Avicenna was a colourful character who travelled from court to court seeking a patron for his genius; sometimes he was in hiding, sometimes in prison! His argument for the existence of God is (Aristotelian) that God is the necessary first cause. Because Avicenna sought an intellectual explanation of God he ended up with a 'god' that is like some concept of theoretical physics not dissimilar to Spinoza's god. This obviously is an altogether different proposition to the intergalactic Dumbledore offered to us by the Abrahamic texts. He was a strict determinist and held that every cause issues an effect in an entirely deterministic way, and since the world turns out to be a necessary emanation from God, if there was another world, then it would be identical to this one in every way. (If I drank a lot and shagged around then I would probably also be attracted to a philosophy in which everything was inevitable). But if everything is necessary then how can we be moral agents choosing between good and evil? Indeed how can moral choices even exist in a deterministic world? Additionally he agreed with Farabi that the Universe was eternal. The theologians were always going to be pissed off.

Al-Ghazali (1058-1111) saw Avicenna as an enemy to be refuted. He felt Avicenna's philosophy (indeed philosophy in general) was incompatible with Islamic faith. His arguments against Avicenna are interesting in that they appear similar to Hume's arguments against causation. Al-Ghazali's concern was that if everything about God is necessary, then it would be a necessary act that God creates us rather than an act of kindness; and that Avicenna therefore posed a challenge to Islam. Al-Ghazali's books tended to have brilliant titles, the most famous of which is *'The Incoherence of the Philosophers'*, in which he stated that since all truth is in the Koran, there is no need of speculation independent of revelation. But then Al-Ghazali had a mental breakdown which he attributed to a crisis of faith and confessed to only being a Muslim verbally. He then spent several years wandering and meditating. In later life he became a devout Sufi, but still produced interesting work. Like Kant he was interested in critiquing reason itself, albeit to justify his cultural prejudices. (Maybe Kant also sought to critique reason to justify his cultural prejudices but at least he tried to do it dispassionately). It seems to me Al-Ghazali was a prodigiously gifted thinker who made the error of applying infinite scepticism to reason but insufficient scepticism to religion. This is all the more erroneous when we consider that religion relies on an appeal to something higher and external to itself, whereas reason does not.

Averroes (1126-1198) (the great commentator on Aristotle) was a believer, but not rigidly orthodox. He said that philosophers alone were qualified to interpret the Koran, and that holy text which contradicted philosophy should be considered as merely allegorical. He held that the world had not been created, and that after death we don't go to heaven but become part of a type of Hegelian universal intellect. When Averroes came across Al-Ghazali's *'The Incoherence of the Philosophers'* he responded with the winningly titled *'The Incoherence of the Incoherence'* in which he referred followers of Al-Ghazali to various commentaries on Aristotle written by ... er ... himself! But Al Mansur had published an edict to the effect that God had decreed hellfire for those who thought that truth could be found by reason. Averroes was accused of cultivating the philosophies of the ancients at the expense of the true faith. He was put on trial, banished and his books were burned.

'The Disgrace of Averroes' al-Mansur banishes Averroes from his court (Louis Figuier 1867). 'The Disgrace of al-Mansur' would be a more appropriate title. Thankfully today, the world reveres the great scholar and has forgotten the intellectual pigmy.

Do you see the pattern that is emerging? The relationship between the great Islamic philosophers and the clerics is one of conflict, not harmony. As Islamic philosophy matured and became more Aristotelian it became increasingly incompatible with religious doctrine. The further the Islamic geniuses pushed their ideas, the more they came into conflict with the clerics. The intellectual investigation and religious conflict appear *directly* proportional, whereas the greatness of the philosophy seems *inversely* proportional to the religious devotion. Within Islamic history there does not seem to be anyone like Augustine, Kant or Leibniz who simultaneously advanced both philosophy *and* theology. Obviously this is a subject that merits a whole book to itself, but that should not discourage us from observing the general pattern: the 'good' were not great and the great were not 'good'.

The great Islamic philosophers were generally looked upon with suspicion by the theologians, and owed their safety (when they were safe) to enlightened patrons. This should come as no surprise to anyone, a belief system by its very nature must be in conflict with the sort of synthetic a posteriori knowledge we find in Aristotle, because synthetic a posteriori knowledge is about learning from observations, whereas belief systems are about unalterable internal values that determine *how* we see. Philosophy is the questions business, religion is the answers business. Philosophy is about wondering, religion is about explaining. Philosophy looks for errors, religion blocks out doubt. Philosophy is about developing ideas, religion feels threatened by ideas. With philosophy new ideas come to us and change us, with religion internal beliefs are projected from us onto the world. Philosophy is about changing our minds, religion is about not changing our minds. Philosophers submit arguments we can accept or reject, theologians impose belief. Philosophy is a series of unique statements, religion uses repetition to train the mind to act automatically without thinking. Philosophy is questions that can't be answered, religion is answers that can't be questioned. Philosophy is about thinking, religion is about not thinking. It is the questions, not the answers that matter most.

Of all the above my least favourite is Al-Ghazali because ultimately he came down on the side of religion. But still Al-Ghazali deserves credit for seeing that he had an either/or choice. Al-Kindi tried to reconcile the philosophy of Aristotle and Islam. Let us call this 'Al-Kindi's Dilemma' - In pursuing this Al-Kindi was wasting his time and his talent looking for square circles. And today we see millions of decent intelligent Muslims wrestling with their own version of Al-Kindi's Dilemma: the gay Muslims, the Muslim feminists, the Muslim figurative artists, the Muslim socialists, the Muslim philosophers, they are all wasting their lives seeking to reconcile two inherently irreconcilable things. When philosophy and religion are in conflict, why not fix the religion? After all religion crushes people, prohibits thought and generates war, whereas philosophy enriches people, cultivates ideas and generates peace.

Now let's consider the two greatest intellectual achievements of the Islamic world – algebra and algorithms. It is clear from the 'Al' prefix, that these ideas came from Islamic societies (unlike 'Arabic' numerals which are actually a Hindu invention). Imagine you are a genius growing up in an Islamic society. To what field of endeavour should you apply your mind? If you apply yourself to philosophy you will attacked by the clerics if you innovate, and forgotten if you don't. Politics, ethics and metaphysics are branches of philosophy so they are out. Art, music and literature are policed by theologians. So what can you innovate without having to live in fear that you could land yourself in trouble? The answer is obviously to work on something completely abstract, where all worldly cultural values are excluded. There is nothing in algebra or algorithms that is obviously Islamic or which the most devout Muslim could object to. For similar reasons the Islamic world has made a far greater contribution to abstract art than representational art.

Now if we consider the field of Chemistry - Empedocles (494-434 BC) claimed that everything was earth, air, fire and water. Following this, the field of chemistry made no significant advance until Islamic chemists began their investigations into alchemy. It would be churlish to deny this great contribution from the Islamic world, but again, we must ask ourselves why these excellent, intelligent Muslims applied themselves to this problem in particular? The answer is obvious: How could any theologian condemn someone for chemistry? Again, knowledge progressed where dogma was absent.

Let's say you disagree with my argument. I'm sure many will. To demonstrate that my argument is wrong you are required to provide lots of examples of philosophers, intellectuals, figurative painters, comedians, campaigners for gay rights, women's rights, democracy, equality, multiculturalism and free speech who were not persecuted by Islamic clerics.

8 – Hume

Here is an extract from David Hume's essay '*Of the Standard of Taste*' in which he discusses the Koran.

"*The admirers and followers of the Alcoran insist on the excellent moral precepts interspersed throughout that wild and absurd performance ... But would we know whether the pretend prophet had really attained a just sentiment of morals? Let us attend to his narration, and we shall soon find that he bestows praise on such instances of treachery, inhumanity, cruelty, revenge, bigotry, as are utterly incompatible with civilised society. No steady rule of right seems there to be attended to, and every action is blamed or praised so far only as it is beneficial or hurtful to the true believers.*"

9 – Schopenhauer

In '*The Will in Nature*' Schopenhauer described Islam as '*detestable*'. This is what he wrote about it in the WWR v.2 (1844) Chapter XVII

'Consider the Koran, for example; this wretched book was sufficient to start a world-religion, to satisfy the metaphysical need of countless millions for twelve hundred years, to become the basis of their morality and of a remarkable contempt for death, and also to inspire them to bloody wars and the most extensive conquests. In this book we find the saddest and poorest form of theism. ... I have not been able to discover in it one single idea of value.'

10 – Nietzsche

Predictably, the only Western philosopher to take a charitable view of Islam is Nietzsche because his is a worldly, power philosophy that is incapable of condemning cruelty.

"Thou goest to women, do not forget thy whip ... Man shall be trained for war, woman for the recreation of the warrior, all else is folly." - Thus Spoke Zarathustra.

11 - Allah Does Not Exist

In this chapter, for shorthand, I will use 'God' as a synonym for Jehovah/Allah and I will reluctantly write it with an upper-case 'G'.

The God presented to us in the Koran is an impossible absurdity. I will explain why using 'necessary reason' and 'sufficient reason'. Obviously, my argument won't impress anyone who does not accept reasoning as valid, but such people have excluded themselves from the conversation anyway.

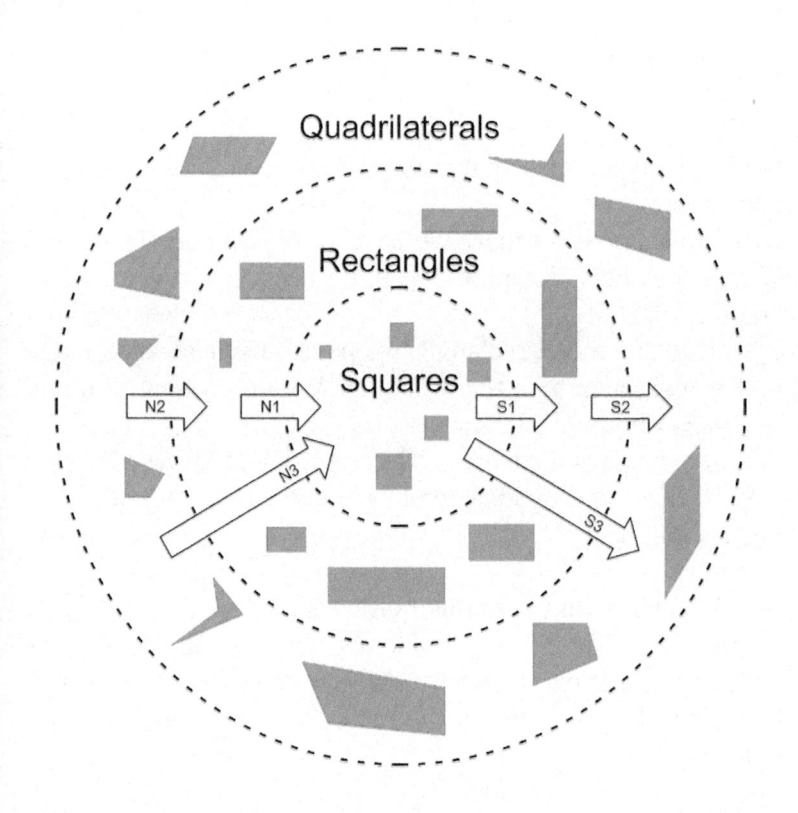

Above is a Venn diagram. The outer ring contains all four-sided shapes (quadrilaterals) the ring inside that contains rectangles and the central ring contains squares. Now let's look at this Venn diagram in terms of necessary and sufficient reason.

We see that the necessary reason flows from the periphery to the centre.
N1 - It is necessary that a shape is rectangle for it to be a square.
N2 - It is necessary that a shape is a quadrilateral for it to be a rectangle.
N3 - It is necessary that a shape is a quadrilateral for it to be a square.

With sufficient reason the flow is from the centre to the periphery.
S1 - If a shape is a square we have sufficient knowledge that it must also be a rectangle. We don't need to know any more about it.
S2 - If a shape is a rectangle we have sufficient knowledge that it must also be a quadrilateral. We don't need to know any more about it.
S3 - If a shape is a square we have sufficient knowledge that it must also be a quadrilateral. We don't need to know any more about it.

So the central ring contains perfect stuff but it's exclusive, whereas the outer ring contains general stuff but it's inclusive. Can you see where this is going? Now let's repeat our Ven diagram, this time with minerals, animals and humans.

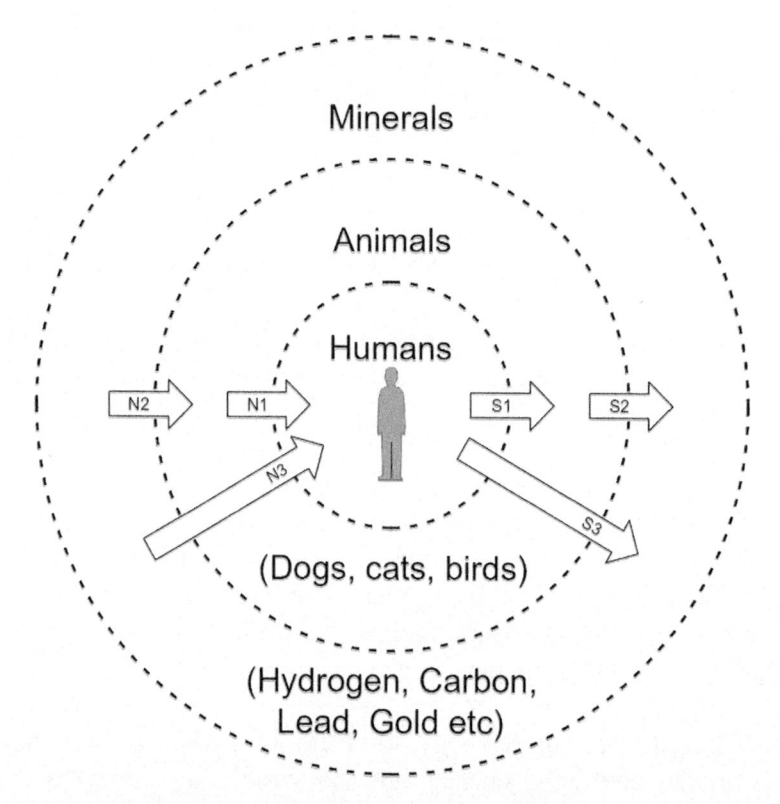

Again, we see the necessary reason flows from the periphery to the centre:

N1 - It is necessary that something be animal for it to also be a human.

N2 - It is necessary that something must be mineral to be animal.

N3 - It is necessary that something be mineral for it to also be human.

And again we see the sufficient reason flows from the centre to the periphery:

S1 - If something is human we have sufficient knowledge to say it is also animal. We don't need to know any more about it.

S2 - If something is an animal, we have sufficient knowledge to say it is also mineral. We don't need to know any more about it.
S3 - If something is human we have sufficient knowledge to say it is also mineral. We don't need to know any more about it.

We see from my Venn diagrams that perfection and universality are mutually exclusive. The more perfect and highly evolved is at the centre - but it is exclusive. The ring at the periphery can be universal only by being inclusive lower life forms, imperfection and dead things. Ethics *declines* towards the periphery.

We could add more rings so it flows: geniuses, humans, animals, elements, energy but that would be unnecessary (sorry about the pun) as it would complicate things graphically and this diagram is sufficient (ouch!) for our purposes.

Now let us be more than charitable to the theists and pretend that God exists. Where should we plonk God on our diagram? It is obvious that *if* God exists there are only two possible places it can go on our diagram – the periphery or centre. Let's consider each of these in turn.

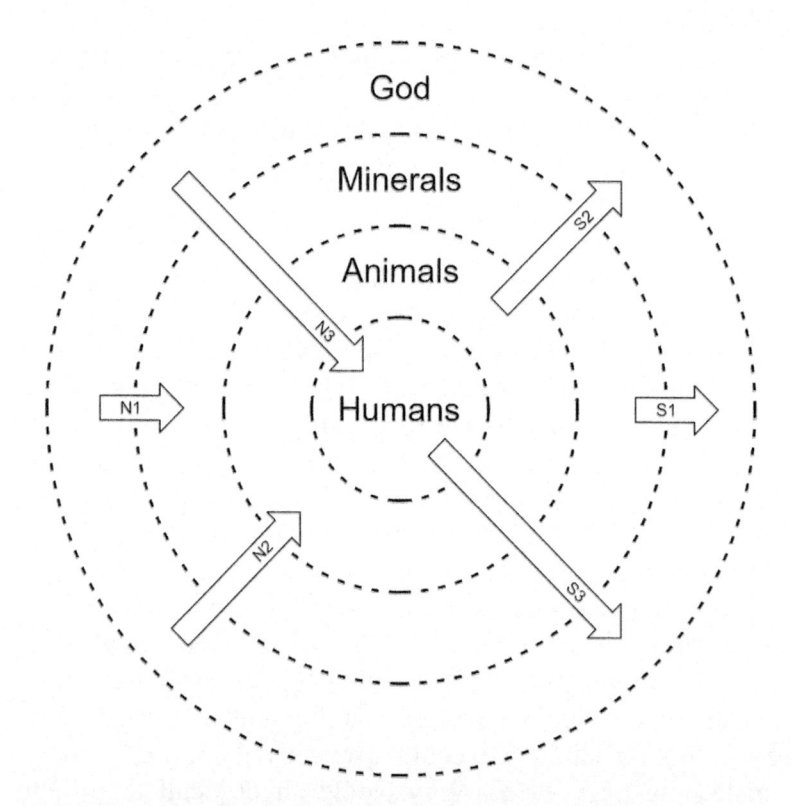

Here is the same Venn diagram, this time with God on the periphery. What type of being is this? What are its attributes? We will start with necessary reason:

N1 - It is necessary that something be God for it to be mineral.

N2 - It is necessary that something be God for it to be animal.

N3 - It is necessary that something be God for it to be human.

Now the sufficient reason:

S1 - If something is mineral we have sufficient knowledge to say it must also be God. We don't need to know anything more about it.

S2 - If something is animal we have sufficient knowledge to say it must also be God. We don't need to know anything more about it.
S3 - If something is human we have sufficient knowledge to say it must also be God. We don't need to know anything more about it.

Let's assume the above Venn diagram describes reality and consider the 'God' thing it presents to us. This God contains all the minerals and energy of the universe, but it is silent, it does not think or communicate (all the reason and ethics takes place within the central ring) it is not ethical, judgemental, jealous or angry. This 'God' is more of a Spinozistic concept of theoretical physics, it bears similarity to Parmenides' *'One'* or Hegel's *'Absolute Idea'* or Leibniz' 'Windowless Monads'. Another good example of this type of deity can be found in Deism (See *'The Age of Reason'* by Tom Paine). But to even call this thing 'God' at all is a misnomer, 'energy' or 'existence' or 'nature' or 'everything' or 'universe' would be more truthful nouns. Indeed there could be no name we could give this thing that's more misleading than *'God'*. Why would anyone call this thing 'God' at all if they weren't a mischievous person seeking to confuse others to accrue power? So this type of 'God' must be rejected by Muslims as it bears no resemblance to the Allah presented to us in the Koran.

I don't believe in God but if I did this would be a pretty good, logically consistent god to subscribe to. This 'God' encourages us to respect all nature, minerals and every living thing. If this were God, then to hurt anyone or disfigure anything would be blasphemy; and to turn any living thing to minerals would constitute an attack on God. Every action of our hands would first entail a moral obligation to leave things more beautiful than we found them.

Now let's consider the alternative possibility. Here is the diagram:

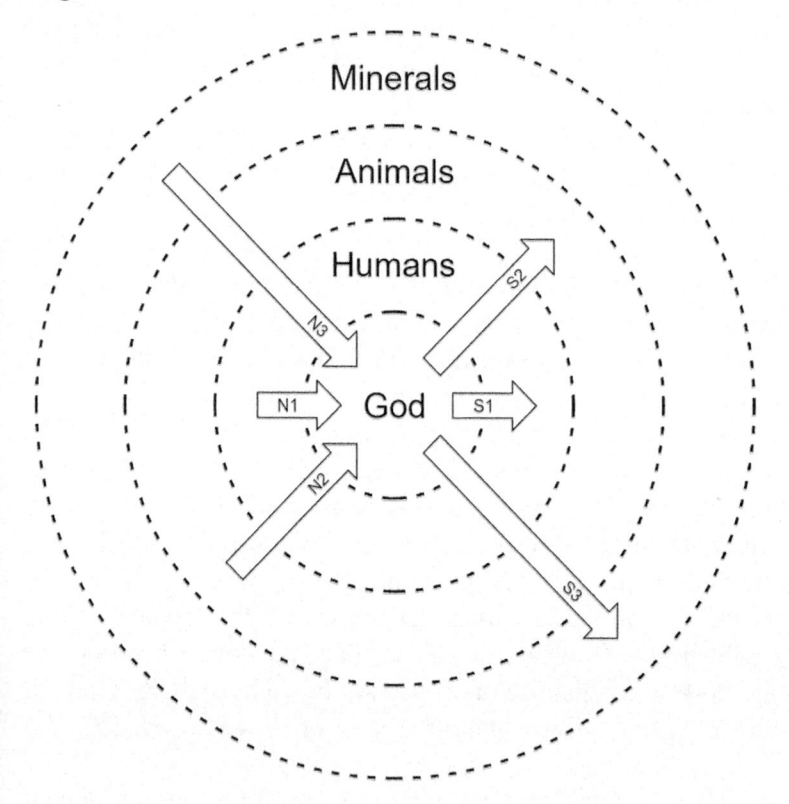

Now we will assume *this* diagram (above) represents reality and see what sort of God it presents to us. First the necessary reason:

N1 – It is necessary for something to be human for it to also be God.

N2 – It is necessary for something to be animal for it to also be God.

N3 – It is necessary for something to be mineral for it to also be God.

Now the sufficient reason:

S1 – If something is God we have sufficient knowledge to know it must also be human. We don't need to know anything more about it.
S2 – If something is God we have sufficient knowledge to know it must also be animal. We don't need to know anything more about it.
S3 – If something is God we have sufficient knowledge to know it must also be mineral. We don't need to know anything more about it.

So what sort of God is this? On the plus side it can be perfect, moral, speak, and love, it is alive, additionally it is highly evolved. The problem is that it is finite, physical, it only exists on earth, in humans, and not necessarily in all humans. It cannot exist where humans don't exist and offers no afterlife outside memory. It can die and is not eternal or omnipotent. The thing that strikes us about this 'god' is how small, local and brief it could be. This 'God' could be one momentary thought in the mind of one person. It is not so much a 'god' as an idea. Examples of this type of thing could be the Nietzschean Superman, the idea of genius, or Aristotle's magnanimous man. Again, why call it 'God' at all? Why not call it '*someone great*' or '*love*' or '*friend*'?

Again, although I'm an atheist this could be a pretty decent 'god' to subscribe to. It is logically consistent, ethical and we can relate to it as human beings. The problem for the theists (again) is that it bears no resemblance to the deity presented to us in the Old Testament, New Testament or Koran.

So intelligence and perfection increases as we go to the centre of our Venn diagram and decline as we go to the periphery; whereas universality and permanence increases towards the periphery and diminishes towards the centre. Thus our Venn diagrams present us with two options: a central 'god' that can be a perfect, living, intelligent moral being but which is not timeless or universal … or a peripheral 'god' that is universal and eternal but not living, ethical or intelligent and includes imperfections. Advocate whichever you like, I don't care, your problem is they are mutually exclusive. The God/Allah/Jehovah presented to us by the Abrahamic texts is a mash up of two things which could not be more dissimilar.

	God - Periphery	God - Centre
Universal	✓	✗
Permanent	✓	✗
Immortal	✓	✗
Intelligent	✗	✓
Ethical	✗	✓
Potentially Perfect	✗	✓
Communicates	✗	✓
Highly Evolved	✗	✓

Both of these concepts of God have characteristics that appeal. The problem is the Old Testament, New Testament and Koran muddle them up. Jews, Christians and Muslims assure us that Jehovah/God/Allah has the impressive attributes of both, but without any of the shortcomings that necessarily arise. The Jehovah/God/Allah their books present to us is oxymoronic: If a god is infinite and eternal it cannot live, think, judge or speak – if it can, then it can't be infinite and eternal.

This is the problem with the ontological argument. The ontological argument asserts that God is perfect, that something that is real must be better than something that is not, therefore God exists. This argument fails because:
1, It assumes God to be both the innermost AND outermost ring, which confounds necessary and sufficient reason.

2, It assumes perfection. Even if we entertain the idea of existence, there is no reason to suppose it is perfect, indeed there are numerous reasons to assume it is very imperfect.

3, The ontological argument assumes perfection and reality to be directly proportional when they are obviously inversely proportional. Geometry and mathematics are perfect precisely because they are abstractions that exclude empirical reality.

… and as Kant observed, most arguments for the existence of God are just the ontological argument rephrased. Some other arguments for the existence of God:

Appeal to beauty. Theists sometimes maintain that the existence of beauty implies the existence of God. But if that argument were valid then by the same argument the existence of ugly things would demonstrate the non-existence of God. So we can put that argument to one side on the grounds of inconsistency.

The first cause argument. Does everything have a cause? Yes or No? If 'yes' then there is infinite regression, no original cause, no creation, no creator, no God. So theists must claim that something can exist which is not caused, and that thing is Jehovah/God/Allah. A convenient exception! If one exception is admitted then why not two or three?

If there is only one uncaused thing and everything else is an inevitable mechanical consequence then there can be no morality because everything appearing to be a moral choice was never a *choice* at all - if 'moral decisions' are caused then they're neither moral *or* decisions! So anyone claiming there is just one first cause automatically disqualifies themselves from moral judgements!

So if morality is real, uncaused things can exist which undermines the idea of a first cause, and if nothing is caused there is no creator. Either way it's looking bleak for the first cause argument. Another problem with the first cause argument is it assumes knowledge about something which (by its very nature) can only be speculated about.

Morality argument. Theist sometimes maintain that religion gave us morality when it is clearly the other way round. Most humans are inherently moral, and religions are the attempt to systematise morality into social systems. Religions tend to be usurped by mischievous people seeking advantage in this world, so they dream up convenient 'gods' to justify their power grabs. Hence the most religious societies tend to be the cruellest.

Appeal to probability. All the evidence of our senses is compatible with Darwinism, none of the evidence of our senses is incompatible with Darwinism. Theists counter that Darwinism is improbable, but however improbable it may be, it will always be *more* probable than the theory that the same ends came about as a consequence of supernatural intervention. Critiques of reason are automatically invalidated by belief in the fantastic. *'Reasonable belief'* is an oxymoron.

Burden of proof. Quibbles about Dawin or Hume do not constitute a credible argument for the existence of God. If you want me to subscribe to your ideology it is incumbent on you to provide me with a reason for doing so. If you offer no plausible explanation as to how creation came about that invalidates your demand that evolution be explained in every detail prior to acceptance.

All of us in our professional lives have to comply with codes of conduct. For example if I were a financial advisor, I could lose my license to practice if I made false or misleading claims. But for Theists it seems the more extravagant their claims, the less evidence is required to support them!

Until Pascal, Theists had a monopoly on education and knowledge. Geniuses like Descartes, Spinoza, Locke and Leibniz seemed to be on their side so they had no problem with reason. But when reason became incompatible with their gods theists claimed there must be a problem with reason itself. This reveals theists to be fair-weather-friends of reason, pretending to value it only so long as it seemed to confirm their beliefs.

Pascall's wager. Pascall's wager is unusual in that it is empirical and difficult to disprove, but that no sincere believer appeals to it. The wager is that belief costs nothing, the rewards (if you are right) are infinite as are the punishments (if you are wrong) so we have nothing to lose and everything to gain from believing. The counter arguments are that it is cynical and could be advanced in the defence of any deity however ludicrous.

Pascal might argue that I must first believe in order to understand the reason for belief, but that seems to be putting the cart before the horse. Before I subscribe to some doctrine I want reason for doing so, my position has the added benefits of (1) not giving a free pass to hucksters and (2) advancing a reasonable philosophy that gives us things like medicine.

Appeal to happiness. This argument is that belief makes life happier and bearable. This is a nice argument that is true for many - so long as belief is voluntary. When involuntary it makes life unhappier and unbearable.

Appeal to order. Similar to the appeal to happiness, but that a creed delivers social order. Order for who? The electors and elected or the chosen ones?

'But it's my religion, my faith, it's what I believe.' This argument we can scrunch up and throw in the dustbin where it belongs. It's true because you *think* it's true? Call that an argument? I call it 'the dictator's prerogative'. What scammer hasn't invoked that old chestnut! Why is it what you believe? Why not fix the belief? The lunacy of Soren Kierkegaard is indistinguishable from that of al-Mansur.

Appeal to higher authority. Appeal to credulity.

The most compelling arguments for religion aren't actual arguments at all. For example, if I walk through any town, what is the most beautiful building? Obviously it's the church. What are the genuinely powerful essays? Well it's hard not to cry when reading the last page of '*The Happy Prince*' by Oscar Wilde. Looking at these things is empirical and meaningful and it would be churlish to dismiss them, but we cannot accept them as valid arguments. Theists must be politely but firmly invited to concede that (with the best will in the world) their belief systems are usurped to incubate horror.

I hope the reader can appreciate that I'm not picking on Islam in particular here. It would be intellectually dishonest of me to condemn the basis of Islam but then say that some other belief system is dandy. There is a problem with belief systems in general. Belief implies we don't know, and knowledge implies we don't believe. Knowledge and belief are mutually exclusive. The former helps, the latter hinders.

If anyone is interested in this subject, then I recommend Bertrand Russell's essays on Leibniz and Kant in '*History of Western Philosophy*'. But the key point I am making in this chapter is that Islam is founded on lies. It is a lie that there is one true god called Allah, it is a lie that Muhammad was his messenger rather than his author; and those who assert otherwise are scammers engaged in a classic power-grab.

12 – When Is A Religion Not A Religion?

Superficially Islam seems similar to other religions. It has praying, a set of rules, a 'holy book', a deity, rules, 'holy' buildings, clerics, congregations, yearly rituals etc. But I assert it is a pretend religion, masquerading as a faith because that is the easiest way to achieve its ultimate objective of domination.

Lots of institutions and ideologies have key texts, prestigious buildings, hierarchical structures, charismatic central figures etc. By what right is Islam exceptional from any other movement? The fact that it involves praying? Praying is a type of thought. Numerous activities entail special types of concentration. Imagine a boxer in the dressing room before a fight, he is shadow boxing, psyching himself up, getting into the right state of mind for the contest. What makes that any different to Islamic 'prayer'? The fact that 'prayer' is directed at some deity? But I have proved that any such deity cannot exist or listen. Praying is asking a fictional character to suspend the laws of physics for my convenience, it is idiotic timewasting; at least meditation allows people to appraise their lives and control their breathing without the ludicrous spiritual mumbo jumbo. The fact that Islam involves prayer does not entitle it to be called a religion any more than any other activity involving thought.

Having disposed of Allah and prayer, I repeat my question. What makes Islam a religion at all? Heaps of outfits have big buildings, funny hats, dietary codes and habits that make no sense, what justifies Islam's claim to exceptional status? The fact that it entails belief? So does stock trading (when it is least profitable). The fact that it induces hysteria? So does football! The fact that it involves contemplation? So does art! I repeat my question and ultimately the answer must be that Islam provides a moral system to live by. The problem is – it doesn't. Here we return to the devastating argument penned, not by myself but by David Hume. Within Islam judgements are made on the basis of act*or* rather than act*ion*. That may be a clear position, but it is not a moral position – it is the opposite of a moral position.

Let's take for example human rights. What is the position of Islam regarding human rights? The answer seems to be that human rights are good when they make more territory more Islamic and bad when they don't. But human rights are (by definition) for humans generally. It is oxymoronic to appeal to them selectively, when it is convenient to do so, claiming them for yourself whilst denying them for everyone else. Appealing to human rights so you can advance your attack on the rights of others is the epitome of hypocrisy. Surely the whole point of a religion is to be ethically consistent?

Within Islam good and bad is determined by the extent to which an action makes more territory more Islamic. This can be demonstrated by the inability of Islamic scholars to give examples of 'good' acts that reduce Islamic domination or 'bad' acts that increase it. What is actually good or bad? It's a practical question. Apparently we should pray to Allah, but why? What is actually *good* about that act? Apparently making the world more Islamic makes it more good because it makes it more Islamic. But that's a circular argument, I'm still awaiting the definition of good and bad. Could it possibly be that these definitions are never produced because they would automatically admit that Islam is not exceptional, goodness need not be Islamic and that many Islamic acts are bad (the mass murder of Jews and Hindus for example).

If the afterlife promised by Islam is so brilliant then why is every act for territorial domination *in this* world? The answer obviously is because Islam is not a religion at all but a military strategy. I would say that a military strategy is about securing territory by whatever means necessary, whereas an ethical code prescribes actions for a more beautiful world irrespective of whether those actions advantage ourselves, specifically, here and now. We may quibble about these definitions and they are not mutually exclusive, but every Islamic action would seem to meet the military rather than the ethical definition. When is a religion not a religion? When it is Islam.

13 - The Character of Muhammad

What attributes should we expect from the author of an ethics document? A good listener? Charitable towards others? Indifference to the social status or cultural backgrounds of others? A disregard of worldly gain? Well read? Compassionate? Forgiving? Respectful of women? Muhammad was an illiterate, polygamous, mass-murdering, slave-owning paedophile, wholly destitute of the qualities we would hope to find in the author of an ethics document. Where are the examples of polite disagreement with those weaker than himself? He set up an apartheid state in which those who disagreed were second class citizens. I see no act that was not ultimately about the conquest of hearts, minds and territory. Every appeal to a higher values was a disingenuous power play to achieve the submission of others *in this* world.

What Muslims call 'divine revelation' I call 'making it up'. Notice how the 'visions' conveniently accord with worldly gain and sexual gratification? As usual 'truth' is whatever it's convenient to believe, we call this 'the dictator's prerogative'.

14 – The Character of Islam

Naturally Islam is in the image of its designer. Muhammad was a warlord, obsessed with the conquest of hearts, minds and territory; so when he created a fictional character called Allah, unsurprisingly Allah had all the attributes a warlord would dream of: he is vengeful, unquestioned, judgemental, indestructible, immortal, all-powerful, merciful to those who obey and merciless to those who don't. We are told he gives infinite rewards to those who put themselves entirely at his disposal. Violence in his name is his name is 'good' otherwise it is 'evil'. Inconvenient questions = enemy propaganda. It is obvious that Allah did not create man – a man created Allah. If I wanted my soldiers to be obedient, hardworking and risk their lives for my project then Allah is exactly the type of deity I would invent for them. Indifferent to suffering, judgemental, bloodthirsty, jealous and obsessed with the sex lives of others, Allah seems to have all the characteristics of the most unpleasant people. More Satan than God, 'Allah' is not only fictional, it's autobiographical.

It naturally follows that from its inception Islam had been concerned with the domination of territory. If we look at the characteristics of Islam, from what point of view do they all make sense? From the point of view of territorial domination. And here I am not just talking about the bombings, stabbings, beheadings, or driving vehicles into crowds of people; virtually every Islamic act, however innocuous it may appear, is a microcosm of Islam's endless world war against the rest of us.

Feminism. Naturally every general will want lots of soldiers as there is strength in numbers. So women are told that silence and obedience are virtues. Their genitals are mutilated because it is easier to impose submission on someone once they have been brutalised.

Women are livestock, commodities, the property of their father until they are the property of their husbands. They are to remain in a compound - if they venture outside they are to be covered with a tarpaulin and walk behind the man. They are not to even shake hands with other men. Educated women have fewer children and ask more questions so women's education is restricted. From what point of view does this cruel discrimination make sense? From the point of view of territorial domination. For example, the head covering is not a stylistic sartorial choice but a partition, a cordoning off, a demarcation of human demographic territory, in a similar way to how a man might put a tarpaulin over his things outside the house. This is exactly what we would expect when society is designed by someone incapable of having a committed relationship to one woman.

Gay rights. Gays tend not to have children, and there is strength in numbers. So to maximise submission Islam decrees homosexuality a sin.

The Jizya tax. This is a tax on *not* being Muslim, it is institutional, financial discrimination – an economic incentive to submit.

Fasting. This is a basic form of military training.

Art. Why do you suppose figurative art is prohibited in Islam? Obviously because it's about thought and questions. Why investigate the nature of humanity when all the answers have already been given? The very act of thinking about the nature of humanity cannot but threaten an ideology claiming to be the last word. This is why only pattern and abstract art are permitted, and why the magnificent sculptures of Buddha were destroyed in Afghanistan. (See also the chapter on Kindi)

Music. The wailing dissonance of Islamic music is a de-rationalising call to arms; its purpose is to induce hysteria.

Around 1976 in New York three types of music were invented – punk, rap and disco. Today these three music forms dominate the world, but how have they fared in the Islamic world? Punk is out because the inherent nature of punk is rebellion, whereas the inherent nature of Islam is submission. An Islamic punk band is an oxymoron. So what of disco? Disco is tolerated only in specific circumstances so long as its theme of gay liberation is suppressed. What about rap (hip-hop)? Rap is fine, partly because it's male dominated, partly because worldly conquest is a central theme, but primarily because rap distils music into just beats and words, so there is nothing inherent in the nature of rap that negates ideas of takeover or territorial domination (love and forgiveness are not hard-wired into the genre) so it's easy for Rap to be a sermon that accords with orthodox doctrine.

Halal meat. This involves cutting the throat of a conscious animal whilst reading some nonsense from the Koran. The aim is to normalise nightmarish slaughter.

Hate masquerading as anti-discrimination. Then there is the war against free speech, the persecution of intellectuals and comedians, and the framing of all criticism as 'hate speech', the selective appeal only to the rights that advance the project and the disregard of rights that don't. Anyone deemed impure suddenly finds themselves cast from society, unemployed and unemployable.

Alcohol. Societies that permit alcohol are obviously superior to those that don't, because drinking is about being sociable, thinking differently and cross-checking stories. This cannot but threaten a dead-end ideology so it is prohibited in Islam.

From what point of view do all the above make sense? From the point of view of territorial domination. Each of the above is an act of micro ethnic-cleansing. Every insistence that we must accommodate and they must be accommodated is a microcosm of the same vast intergenerational attack. No

Islamic leader ever says *"Women should dress however they like"* or *"I support gay rights!"* or *"Free speech? Fine by me!"* because if they did they wouldn't be an *Islamic* leader.

When I was young the Islamic war was something in another continent. Now people are being stabbed at the end of my street. My employer sends me emails about Ramadan pressuring me to conduct myself in an inoffensive way. At work, social life is dying out - it's a political minefield to organise a social event because those who don't drink might claim they're excluded. Indeed, to even discuss the subject, to even say the word 'Islam' is to find oneself in a conflict situation. The above are all microcosms of the same general program of submission.

15 – General Demographics.

Islam subjugates women, to have more children, to numerically dominate. So, any group adjacent to an Islamic community must have more children or find itself outnumbered. Consequently, China has abandoned it's one child policy and modern Hindu culture emphasises masculinity. To the Westerner, contemporary Hindu culture appears misogynistic, but what do you suppose Hindus make of Westerners sterilising their own children and fetishising infertility? Ultimately, we are submitting, Hindus aren't.

The human race is having to be ever more ingenious to feed a growing population with less labour. This is driven in no small part by Islam regarding demographics as an arms race.

16 – Separation of Powers

John Locke (in his second treatise) proposed the separation of state powers. His idea was that the church, executive, legislature, judiciary, police etc all be independent entities. This has made Western governments less decisive than they would otherwise be, but these checks and balances have also been enormously successful in limiting how disastrously bad leaders fail. Islamic societies (naturally) are in the image of their designer and Muhammad was a polymath. He was chief judge, head of the church, head of state and head of the army. Unsurprisingly when we look at the various departments in Islamic societies, we see they are not separate entities, but different branches of a single organism – the church/army. Consequently within every Islamic society, clerics are unelected rulers/dictators/generals with all the social failure that inevitably comes from that. In the West the church and the army are separate, within Islam they are the same thing.

Across the world Muslims are migrating from societies designed by Muhammad to societies designed by Locke. They want to retain their beliefs but not the wasteland it generates - the opportunities, prosperity and meritocracy of the Lockean society, but without admitting that Locke's philosophy is superior to Muhammad's. How is this not hypocrisy? From what point of view is this ethically consistent? Here we return (again) to the argument of David Hume. It is only ethically consistent if we conflate 'making more territory more Islamic' with 'good'. Hypocrites or Invaders, take your pick. A counter argument could be that a philosophy can be socially catastrophic whilst having merit ethically or metaphysically (eg Nietzsche or Plato). But Islam's social failure is *generated* by its ethical failure; its social wasteland is a necessary consequence of its intellectual wasteland.

17 – Failure Export Cycle

Every Islamic state goes through a cycle. There is the initial Islamic ingress either through immigration or outright invasion. Having achieved a foothold, Islam sets up military bases. These may be called 'charities' 'youth clubs' 'summer camps' 'community groups' mosques, sharia courts or they may be pretend human rights groups. Naturally they will claim to be innocuous/virtue incarnate, but every act of each of these groups will ultimately be to make more territory more Islamic. Once the non-Muslims have been ethnically cleansed the economy will collapse for reasons already set out.

Naturally Muslims want to migrate away from their failed societies. It's completely understandable they should seek a functional society to incubate their dysfunctional ideology, the problem is their denial. If you reject war, you are obliged to reject its cause. It is intellectually dishonest to emigrate from a collapsed society but still subscribe to the ideology that *caused* the collapse. This explains the endless emigration *from* Islamic societies throughout history. Emigrate, set up bases, destroy, repeat.

(Non-Muslims never migrate to Muslim majority countries unless they are neo-capitalist tax-dodgers.)

18 – Submission = Good?

If making more territory more Islamic is conflated with morality, then what horror is off-limits? None. Any monstrosity can be excused as long as more submission of more people was the intention. So Islam has not, cannot, and will not peacefully coexist; it presents us with an anti-morality that is only restrained by the fundamental human decency of the Muslims themselves.

19 – Strongmen

When confronted with an ideology that appeals to human rights to advance its attack on human rights, which appeals to multiculturalism to advance its monoculturalism, it's easy to see why non-Muslims feel their compassion is being cynically exploited by invaders obsessed with territorial domination. This is the inherent problem with Locke, so throughout the West we seem to be in an 'age of the strongmen' by which I mean we are transitioning from Lockean to Hobbesian systems.

Hobbes took a dark view of human nature: We are engaged in a struggle of all against all. He saw anarchy as the greatest social ill and advocated top-down power with minimal rights. By contrast Locke took a more positive view of humanity, he saw tyranny as the greatest social ill, advocated bottom-up power and extensive rights. Yes, his system would be more anarchic than Hobbes' but human beings are fundamentally good so catastrophe would be avoided by the separate state departments maintaining a dynamic equilibrium like planets. (He was writing just after Newton and Leibniz had solved calculus, so this idea was vogue).

FULL DISCLOSURE: by instinct I *want* Locke to be right.

In the US, Harris has just lost to Trump in the 2024 election. Harris took a Lockean positive view of human nature (immigration is high, but they are humans, we can make it work) whereas Trump took a darker, misanthropic, Hobbesian view (We are under attack, our choice is defeat or victory). We are embracing ethically degenerate politicians because, however bad they are, at least they're not naïve, and when the naïve man meets the cynical man, the naïve man must wake up or submit. Thus Islam presents the West with a unique challenge: if we cannot make Hobbes democratic, we must make Locke cynical.

20 – Denial

It is extraordinary the lengths people will go to deny the problem of Islam, and I use the word '*deny*' deliberately because it is textbook denial in the Freudian sense.

Trans campaigners who are hypersensitive about what pronouns we use are collectively silent about the institutional homophobia of the Islamic world. People describing themselves as 'feminists' are collectively silent about Islamic patriarchy. Animal rights campaigners who pontificate about the virtues of 'dairy free' say nothing about halal meat which involves the cruel and ritualistic slaughter of animals. Then we have the 'peaceniks' who don't seem to have anything to say about Islam's intergenerational world war against the rest of humanity. The list goes on. Environmentalists who in their daydreams imagine themselves heroic revolutionaries are curiously silent about Islamic economies monetising territory. There are the 'socialists' who remain silent about Islamic ideology being far-right by every conceivable measure. Then we have the silent geniuses who seem to know everything except how to talk clear. The 'anti-discrimination' activists who pontificate about the evils of hate speech but say nothing about Islam's supremacist monoculturalism. The students of colonialism who don't seem to have noticed we are being colonised. Then we have the most fearless and heroic of all the radicals: the 'anti-racism campaigners'. Notice how 'anti-racism activists' always conclude everything is the fault of honkeys? It's almost as if they suffer from precisely the mental illness they're so quick to diagnose in others. Notice how they are silent about Muhammad being a slave owner? When it comes to Islam's involvement in the slave trade suddenly their interest in history evaporates. These 'anti racism activists' are pretend historians who see prejudice only when it confirms their own prejudice. They deliberately conflate disagreeing with Islam with racism because this allows them to pretend their denial is some heroic moral stand. Courageous only against the tolerant, scorn is all I have for the pretend radicals.

Across the Western world birth rates are falling below the 2.1 children per woman necessary for a stable population. So why are 'ambitious' targets being set for housebuilding? If birthrates are going down why build more houses? Our beautiful landscape is being cleared to accommodate the Sharia influx. The 'Green Belt' is being reclassified 'Grey Belt' prior to its annihilation by developers. Millions of plants and animals will die to make way for 'eco-homes'. Do we admit there is a population crisis? Do we admit there is an Islam crisis? No, because that would require courage, so instead the siren voices tell us there is a 'housing crisis'.

It costs more to keep someone in prison than to send them to public school. Prison overcrowding is a huge drain on resources. If you admit millions of people who subscribe to an ideology designed by a mass-murderer, naturally there will be more crime. But it seems we would rather bankrupt ourselves building prisons and laying on elaborate counter terrorism systems than admit there is an Islam crisis, so the siren voices claim there is a *'prisons crisis'*. We are inventing catch phrases like *'housing crisis'* and *'prison crisis'* and *'pension crisis'* and *'the far right are against immigration'* to help us deny the Islam crisis. The denial has become so absurd, it seems people would rather be antisemitic than admit there is a problem with Islam.

I admit I'm generalising about large complex issues, but the size and complexity of these issues is discouraging us from simply observing the obvious pattern. There is no need for a laborious preamble about definitions when the overall pattern is clear as day - Islam advances because non-Muslims are collectively in denial about the menace it poses.

The king is in the altogether. Islamic ideology is an intellectual car crash. Islam is the zombie apocalypse that no one makes a film about, it's the dystopian novel that isn't fiction, the cult that got away with it. If I wanted to create maximum war and stupidity I could do no better than Muhammad. Followers of Islam literally bash their heads against the floor! I was considering writing a comedy spoof of Islam, but I don't have the talent - even Voltaire would struggle to write a parody more ludicrous than the real thing.

21 – Imposters.

The pretend radicals are engaged in a masquerade, the soundtrack is left but the movie is right, naturally they will accuse me of the same thing so how should a reasonable disinterested person decide between us? Simple. Use the tried and tested scientific method of empirical observation. What do the imposters offer? Monoculturalism, patriarchy, homophobia, war, censorship, thought police, environmental destruction and cruelty to animals. I advance the opposite.

22 – Lack of Criticism

Around the world professors mark essays and critique ideas. They critique Marxism, capitalism, modernism, postmodernism, etc. It seems every thinker, every idea is up for debate, except the one which most requires it! Why is there zero critique of the book that makes the most wars? And of course it's the other way round ... the Koran makes the most wars precisely *because* it isn't critiqued. If Islamic ideas have merit, why is critique forbidden? Again, it's the other way round – Islam forbids critique precisely *because* it is an intellectual basket case. If it were subject to a fraction of the analysis applied to Marxism or capitalism, then it would lie in ruins. Its success lies not in advancing good arguments but *preventing* good arguments. For example, no one will die because of this book (except perhaps myself) but countless millions have died because of the Koran. Which of the two books will *you* critique?

When critique of Marxism is prohibited, it goes berserk.
When critique of Capitalism is prohibited, it goes berserk.
When critique of Christianity is forbidden, it goes berserk.
When critique of Islam is forbidden, it goes berserk.
Prohibition of critique incubates fanaticism. What sort of people find this attractive? Cynical people who desire the submission of others.

The main obstacle regarding the problem of Islam is not that we can't solve it, but that even good, intelligent people deny the problem even exists. Islam seems to induce a type of social psychosis whereby it is indulged out of politeness until it is indulged out of fear.

23 – Beliefs Fail

So the problem of Islam isn't just a problem for Islam, if it was it wouldn't matter, we could just leave it to collapse, but unfortunately, Islam is a problem for us all. We have two groups – Islamic societies exporting people and non-Islamic societies importing them. What do both groups have in common? Denial about the failure of belief.

Muslims generally emigrate to states that are not Islamic because they seek a functional society to incubate their dysfunctional ideology. They are so stuck in their beliefs this is actually the easier path – they would rather move across the world than admit there is a problem with their perfect religion.

For the host societies, 'human rights' and 'aid' and 'welfare' are synonyms for 'good'. These programs were set up with the best will in the world, so surely they make the world better not worse, right? It's inconceivable that ethical programs could be usurped for the advancement of tyranny right? Host societies are incapable of admitting their precious institutions have become trojan horses for rottenness, so they cast around for explanations. Apparently, those who disagree are 'racists' the 'far-Right' or 'fascists' (whichever brain-freezing pseudo-description takes your fancy) we need more people because of the pensions crisis, and it's all our fault anyway because of colonialism. The closer and bigger the Islamic war gets the more ludicrous the excuses we make for it. The more it fails the more lofty the claims of moral superiority, and the more vitriolic the blame of everyone – except those who deserve it.

So it would be unfair of me to simply lay the blame for everything at the door of Islam. The deeper problem is that Islam exploits something that is wrong with us. Our rights and welfare systems are founded on an admirably optimistic view of humanity, which assumes invaders will not cynically game the system to achieve conquest. You and I are desperate for that optimistic view to be true, the easy path for everyone is to say it's true. So as Islam advances, and non-Muslims retreat everyone assures everyone else that there is no problem and accuses nay-sayers of heresy. But there *is* a problem and the longer we delude ourselves the bloodier the reconning will be.

24 – How Islam Advances

If Islam is such a second-rate ideology, why does it prosper? Because we incubate it. Islam advances not through its virtues but through our vices:

1, We buy oil.
2, We take holidays in Islamic states.
3, We send Islamic states economic aid for failing.
4, We accept Islamic immigrants without limit, lavish them with free housing healthcare and welfare, and pay them to have children.
5, We are polite about their failed system and apologise for our superior system.
6, We bankrupt ourselves arranging welfare and counter terrorism systems would not be needed if the immigrants were Hindu, Buddhist Taoist, Zen, Jewish, Atheist or pretty much any other denomination.

Spot the pattern? Islam is a prospers because non-Muslims *pay* for it to prosper. Because Islam is a failed social system, left to its own devices it would collapse as every caliphate has done. The reason why it isn't collapsing now is because we are paying this inferior intellectual system to attack us. We bankrolling an ideology pathologically opposed to human rights … in the name of human rights! Not only are we not defending our splendid culture, we are actually assisting our thuggish assailants in their conquest! This is collective social suicide.

25 - Loonies

In virtually every country the Muslim population is increasing. If non-Muslims in those societies regard this an attack then they are not tilting windmills - they are observing empirical reality and expressing reasonable concerns as to its cause. This seems a perfectly empirical scientific method to me. Now let's contrast these Islam sceptics with the climate deniers, trans campaigners, Islam welcomers, flat-earthers and Darwin sceptics. The difference between all those loonies and the Islam sceptics is that the crackpots are generally concerned to deny observable empirical reality.

26 – The War On Empiricism

The modern world was designed by Rousseau and Kant. This subject would require a whole book to itself, but basically Rousseau emphasised feeling over reason, the heart over the head; Kant took that up and created 'Transcendental Philosophy' in which all morality and knowledge is internally determined by the 'thing-in-itself' (Kant's pedantic name for the soul). Kant categorised everything into '*Noumenal*' (supreme, primary, moral) and '*Phenomenal*' (Secondary, Newtonian, worldly). This philosophy now dominates the world and much good has come from it, but the problem is that it has led to a downgrading of empiricism. For example the trans debate comes straight form Kant who called transcendental, that which transcends empirical observation. If gender is what we subjectively believe, rather than what we empirically observe, if we admit that, then why not a thousand other absurdities? Maybe the temperature isn't *really* what the thermometer says, maybe the Earth isn't *really* round, maybe humans didn't *really* evolve from monkeys. If this was just a silly trans joke it wouldn't be a problem; but what *is* a problem is the worldwide war against empiricism. Man is turning the planet into a wasteland, but the destruction is simply allowed to continue. An entire Islamic world war is being waged that is not even discussed! So two deserts are expanding, one environmental, the other Islamic, 'Republicans' deny the existence of the former 'Democrats' deny the existence of the latter. We seem to be prisoners of our feelings, as incapable of admitting there is a problem as we are of admitting guilt or letting go of our first love. At every turn the description used is the one which most totally misrepresents the reality. Men are 'women', women 'men', those who reject Islam are called the 'far-Right', monocultural invasion is called 'multiculturalism', desertification is 'progress' etc.

27 – Concealment

Within Islam images of Muhammad are forbidden, figurative art is forbidden, women are concealed and the Haj is a covered box you don't look inside. Why Islam's emphasis on concealment? I think it is because our imaginations make what's unknown, the repository of our most extreme hopes, fears and desires. Our imaginations generate hysteria, whereas observing empirical reality tends to do the opposite. Naturally those who prosper through derangement will gravitate to secrecy and will use words like 'mystery' and 'sacred' and tell us we cannot know the most important things. So Islam's problem with empiricism isn't restricted to censorship of ideas, discussion of The War or critique of its social failure, across the board observation is forbidden.

28 – Egypt

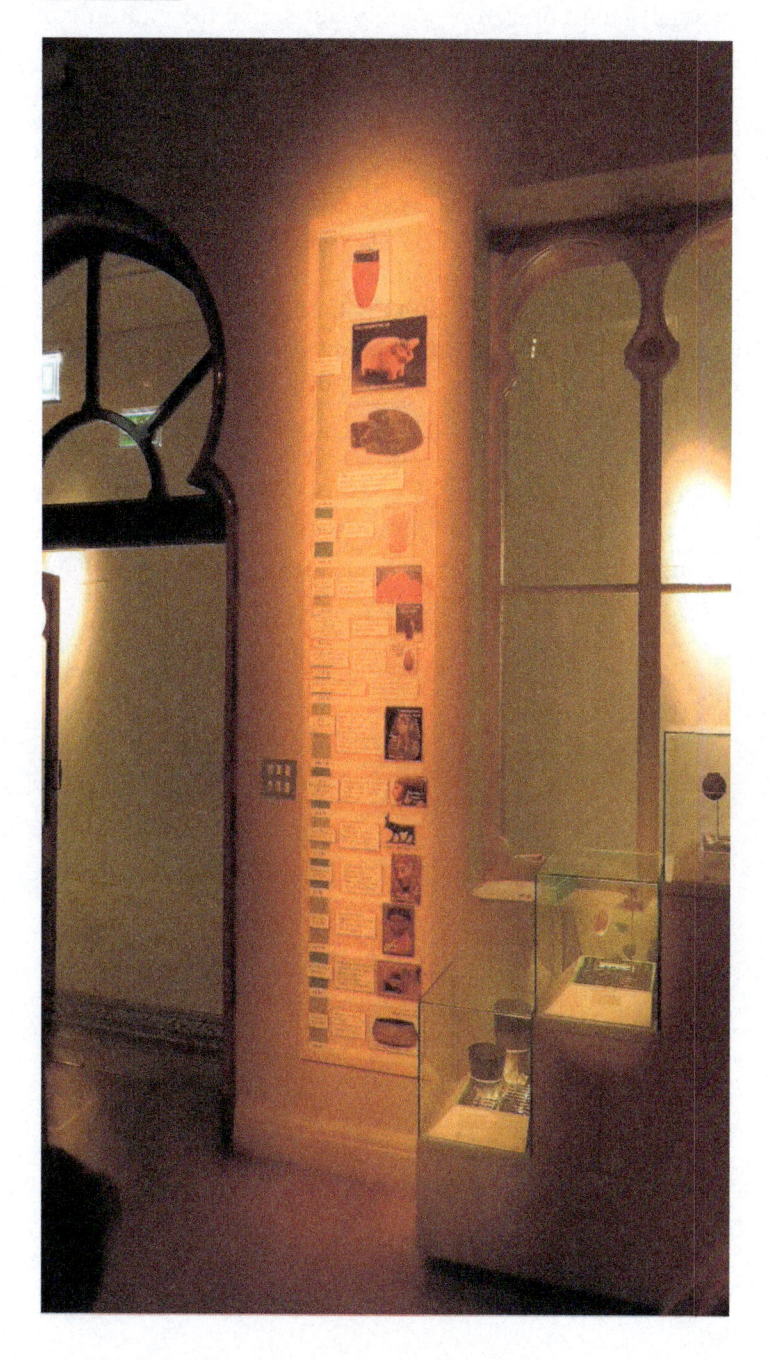

To see what Islam does to a society, let's take the example of Egypt. Egyptian culture had a thousand-year head start on the rest of the human race. The Nile gave Egypt fertile land, it was well connected to the Mediterranean. Egyptians built libraries and schools and pioneered mathematics. Every school child knows Pythagoras' Theorem, it's maybe the most famous geometrical rule in history. But Pythagoras' Theorem was actually an Egyptian invention that Pythagoras used to found Greek Philosophy. So here we have a culture with fertile land, intellectual endeavour, highly organised society and of course, great architecture, centuries before the rest of humanity.

In my local museum there is a chart on the wall of the Egypt room listing the great cultural ages of Egypt. It runs chronologically *from* top *to* bottom. So it begins at the top (5300 BC) showing early ceramics …

4000 BC

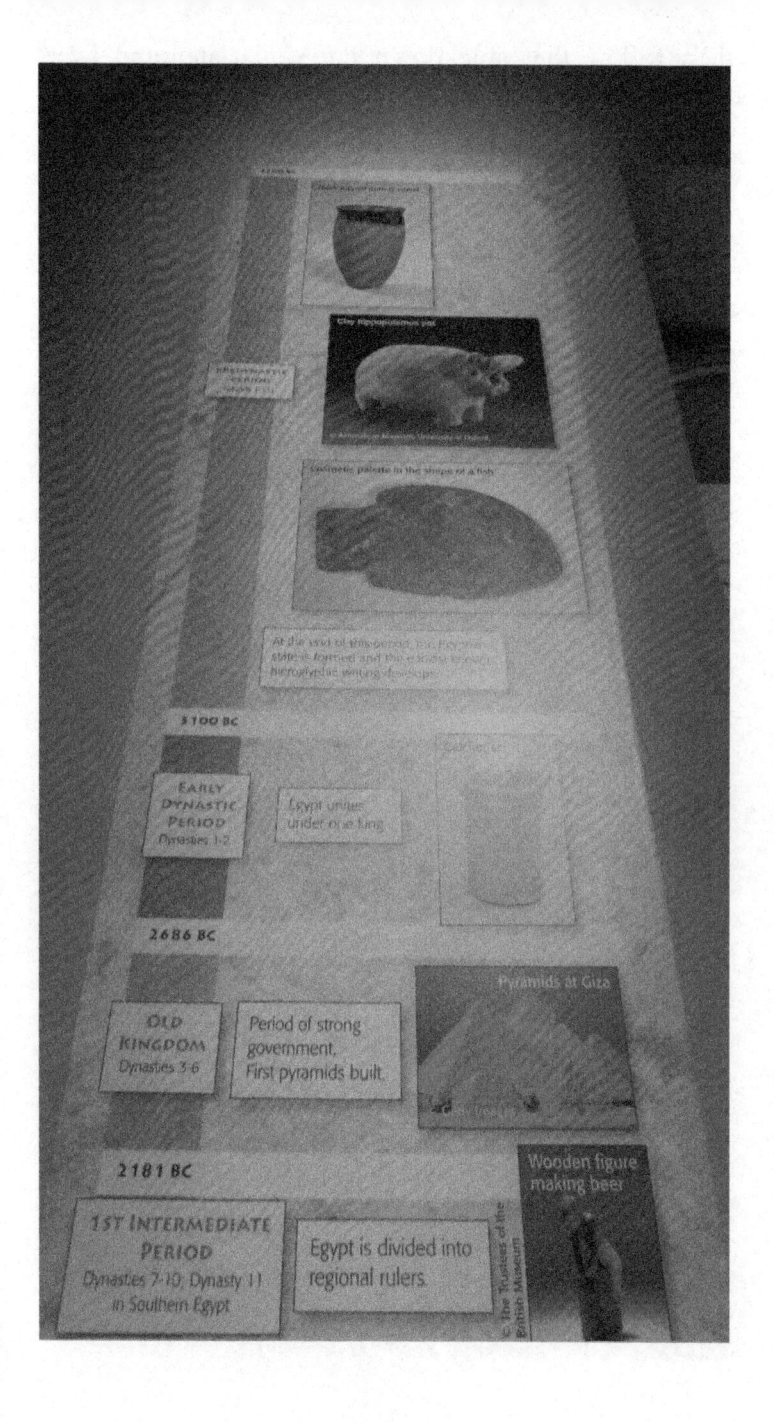

Clay pot in form of a vessel

Clay hippopotamus pot

Cosmetic palette in the shape of a fish

At the end of this period, the Egyptian state is formed and this is also known as hieroglyphic writing develops.

3100 BC

EARLY DYNASTIC PERIOD
Dynasties 1-2

Egypt unites under one king

2686 BC

OLD KINGDOM
Dynasties 3-6

Period of strong government. First pyramids built.

Pyramids at Giza

2181 BC

1ST INTERMEDIATE PERIOD
Dynasties 7-10; Dynasty 11 in Southern Egypt

Egypt is divided into regional rulers.

Wooden figure making beer

We then follow the table down the wall (later and later) through the construction of the pyramids …

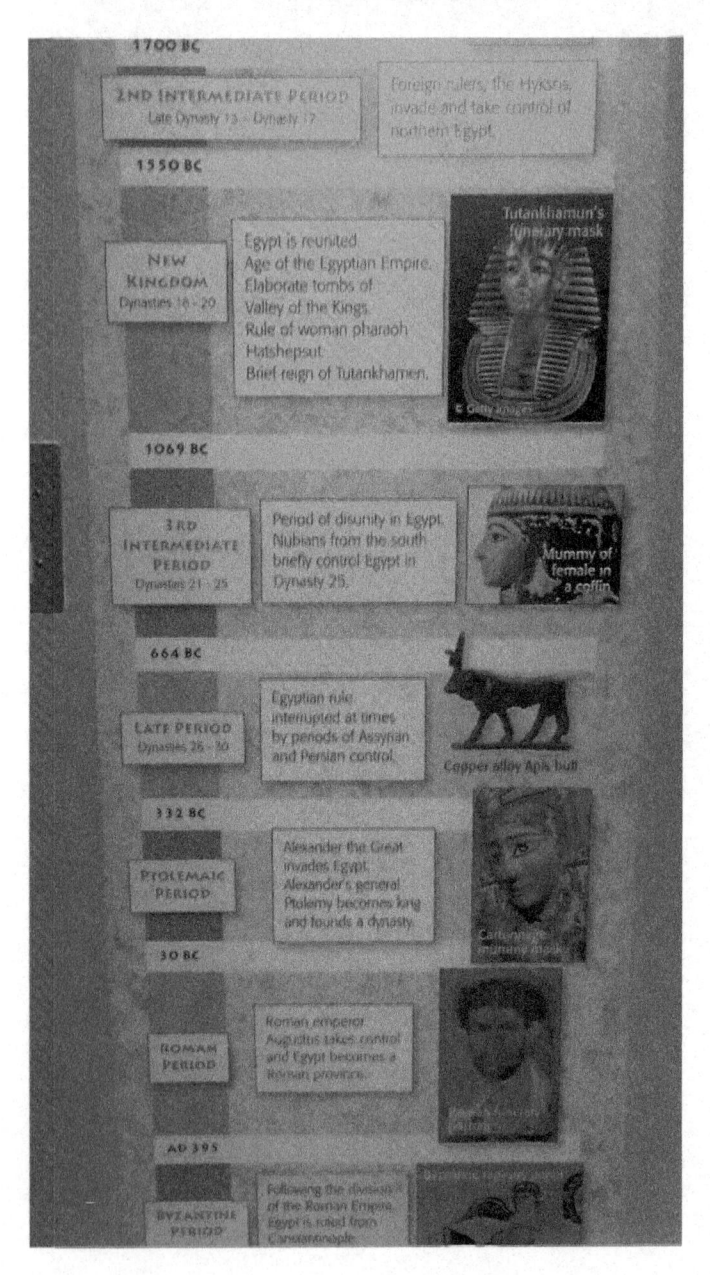

1700 BC

2ND INTERMEDIATE PERIOD
Late Dynasty 13 – Dynasty 17

Foreign rulers, the Hyksos, invade and take control of northern Egypt.

1550 BC

NEW KINGDOM
Dynasties 18 – 20

Egypt is reunited.
Age of the Egyptian Empire.
Elaborate tombs of
Valley of the Kings.
Rule of woman pharaoh
Hatshepsut.
Brief reign of Tutankhamen.

Tutankhamun's funerary mask

1069 BC

3RD INTERMEDIATE PERIOD
Dynasties 21 – 25

Period of disunity in Egypt.
Nubians from the south briefly control Egypt in Dynasty 25.

Mummy of female in a coffin

664 BC

LATE PERIOD
Dynasties 26 – 30

Egyptian rule interrupted at times by periods of Assyrian and Persian control.

Copper alloy Apis bull

332 BC

PTOLEMAIC PERIOD

Alexander the Great invades Egypt.
Alexander's general Ptolemy becomes king and founds a dynasty.

Cartonnage mummy mask

30 BC

ROMAN PERIOD

Roman emperor Augustus takes control and Egypt becomes a Roman province.

AD 395

BYZANTINE PERIOD

Following the division of the Roman Empire, Egypt is ruled from Constantinople.

… the pharaohs, Tutankhamun, the alliance with Rome, Cleopatra, the Byzantine period, then finally at the bottom we have the Islamic conquest. That's it.

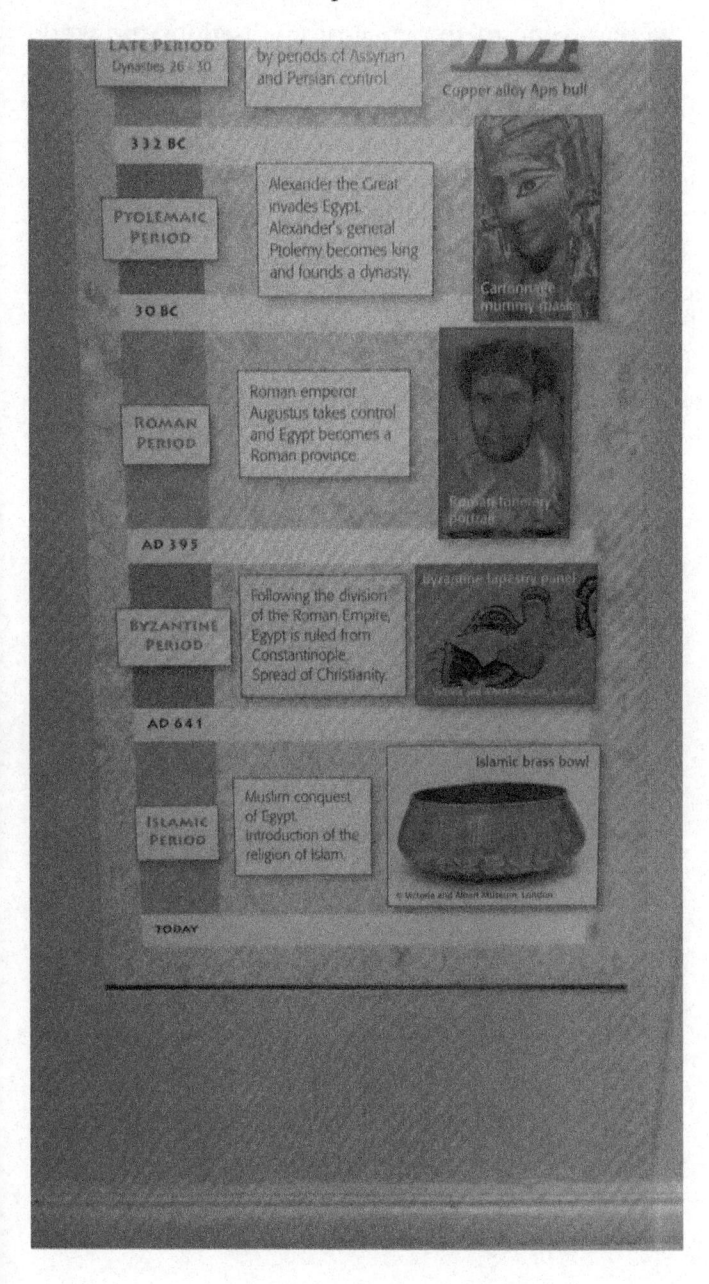

LATE PERIOD Dynasties 26-30	by periods of Assyrian and Persian control	Copper alloy Apis bull
332 BC		
PTOLEMAIC PERIOD	Alexander the Great invades Egypt. Alexander's general Ptolemy becomes king and founds a dynasty.	Cartonnage mummy mask
30 BC		
ROMAN PERIOD	Roman emperor Augustus takes control and Egypt becomes a Roman province.	Roman funerary portrait
AD 395		
BYZANTINE PERIOD	Following the division of the Roman Empire, Egypt is ruled from Constantinople. Spread of Christianity.	Byzantine tapestry panel
AD 641		
ISLAMIC PERIOD	Muslim conquest of Egypt. Introduction of the religion of Islam.	Islamic brass bowl
TODAY		

Here is the photo of the bottom of the wall. I've deliberately not cropped it so we see the skirting board underneath.

So here we have one of the greatest civilisations the world had ever seen, with resources, intellectual excellence, connections and sophisticated social structures, thousands of years ahead of the rest of humanity. There was no reason why Egypt should not continue to be at the forefront of human endeavour. What went wrong? It became an Islamic state. The Byzantines and Christians were ethnically cleansed and for the next 1500 years Egypt produced zero cultural achievements of note. Egyptian culture was great *before* the Islamic conquest, and an intellectual wasteland *afterwards*. Ditto Persia, and soon ditto Europe unless we turn things around.

29 – Freedom of Religion.

Imagine you told the shopkeeper or tax man it was against your religion to pay. Imagine if you told officials or governors, you were not bound by any rule outside your holy book. You would quickly find your 'right' to religious freedom was not without qualifications.

The architects of human rights were careful to caveat *'freedom of religion'*. In his Letter Concerning Toleration, Locke made clear we should be tolerant of religions *provided they reciprocate*. He argued religions *"have no right to be tolerated by the Magistrate ... for by this means the Magistrate would give way to the settling of a foreign jurisdiction in his own country, and suffer his own people to be listed, as it were, for soldiers against his own government."*

Rousseau agreed. In his conclusion to The Social Contract, he wrote: *"... tolerance should be given to all religions that tolerate others, so long as their dogmas contain nothing contrary to the duties of citizenship. Anyone who ventures to say: 'Outside the Church is no salvation' should be driven from the state"*. This was restated almost verbatim in Article X of the 1789 Declaration of the Rights of Man: *"No man ought to be molested on account of his opinions, not even on account of his religious opinions, provided his avowal of them does not disturb the public order established by law."*

It's unpleasant to have to write it, but we cannot admit those who desire our submission - to do so would result in no one having any rights at all.

30 – Sectarianism

Like Protestantism, Islam has splintered into numerous sects, this is for the same reason as Protestantism: Whereas Catholicism has a central authority (Pope in Vatican) Islam and Protestantism are about the relation each human has with a key text, naturally there are as many interpretations as there are interpreters. This explains Islam's sectarian tendencies. So, if you ever wondered why the Islamic world is united in hating Jews but implacably opposed to welcoming refugees from Palestine that's why. Funding Palestinians to kill Jews is one thing, welcoming them as brothers, quite another.

Note: Israel has a stark choice: win or lose. If they win Slavoj Žižek will accuse them of being 'shameless' if they lose, they die. Personally, I would choose 'shameless' all day long. Professor Žižek is very clever (he knows all about Hegel) but if he is *so* clever ... how come genius doesn't seem to have spotted the world war?

31 – Mercantilism

I have said that Islamic economies tend to be mercantilist but what does this mean? Mercantilism is an economic policy designed to maximise exports and minimise imports. It sees the world in terms of 'us' and 'them' and seeks to maximise the accumulation of resources, as leverage for one-sided trade. Traditionally this has led to war and colonialism. It's not hard to see why Islam and mercantilism are easy bedfellows. Oil, people, ideology, everything about Islam is about exporting. What does Islam import? Ideas? No. Money? Yes. Super-rich tax-dodgers? Yes. Tourists? Yes - on the proviso that they spend, leave soon and have no rights.

32 – Pre-emptive Retaliation

I don't want to bog things down pre-emptively refuting every hypothetical disagreement, but a few are worth dealing with to save time.

1, Belief-based arguments are inadmissible. If you claim something is the case because you *believe* it, then how do we know you are not:

A, Mistaken.
B, Insincere.
C, Both.

Belief and knowledge are mutually exclusive. Belief implies you don't know, and knowledge implies you don't believe. To admit belief-based arguments as valid opens the door to a dictatorship of petulant spasms.

Apparently *"whoever disbelieves in Allah, His angels, His books, His messengers, and the Last Day has certainly gone far astray."* La di da, well that's exactly what I would say if I were a mass murderer seeking to instil obedience in my underlings. Anyone who *believes* has certainly gone far astray from reason, and reason trumps belief because belief must appeal to something outside/above itself (scripture/authority) whereas reason does not.

2, Fact checking. If you think the supreme being transformed into a bird that dictated the ultimate ethics document to an illiterate person, or that Muhammad flew to the moon on a winged horse, then please spare me the lecture about fact checking.

3, Critique is ok. Another attack I expect is that I am not well educated enough to be entitled to an opinion. How much am I required to study before I'm allowed to notice a thousand-year-old world war? Mischievous people could endlessly say I am first required demonstrate understanding of Heidegger (to their satisfaction) prior to having an opinion on anything. Do they *genuinely* desire enlightenment? Or am I being sent on an existential wild goose chase to shut me up? We are only talking about Islam here, it's not as if it's a subject that merits serious investigation.

4, Generalising is valid. I am allowed to say summer is warmer than winter because (though not always true) it is *generally* true. There is something fundamentally wrong with Islam *itself* so there's no need to bore everyone about nuances between Sunnis, Shiites, Sufis and Alawites. If you don't like inductive reasoning, take it up with Francis Bacon.

Because my arguments are based on general observations if anyone is going to disagree with them, I'll automatically suspect they are either an interested party or scared of admitting I am right.

5, Offense. Accusations of 'offense' are irrelevant for the following reasons:
1, Copernicus, Galileo and Darwin were deemed offensive. The salient point is not whether propositions are offensive, but whether they are valid/useful/true, and we can leave history to decide that.
2, Many find censorship offensive, so if you think offensive things should be censored then you are damned by your own argument.
3, If what offends you counts, but what offends others doesn't, then that's 'the dictators prerogative' again.
4, How do we *know* you are offended? Prove it. Maybe you are just feigning offense to silence inconvenient truth.

6, Islamophobia. A phobia is an irrational fear, and there is nothing irrational about fearing Islam. Islamophobia is therefore virtually non-existent. It is just a word invented by people who are democracy-phobic, free-speech-phobic, feminism-phobic, homophobic, animal-rights-phobic, art-phobic and multiculturalism-phobic (etc) to pre-emptively silence inconvenient arguments. Notice how people who toss 'Islamophobia' around never critique Hindu-phobia, antisemitism, Buddha-phobia, Christian-phobia in the Islamic world? It's because they've given up trying to produce an argument, so they seek to advance their power grab by accusing those who disagree of mental illness. Every accusation of Islamophobia automatically proves why fear of Islam is not irrational.

So I'm expecting apologists for tyranny (feigning gravitas) to say I should shut up because I'm incorrect, offensive or destabilising; but those criticisms could be applied just as easily to the Koran – and with greater justification! Do they tell the Imans to shut up? Judge on the basis of <u>act</u>ion rather than <u>act</u>or or explain your discrimination.

33 – Quibble All You Like

You can breezily wave your hand and scoff about how ignorant I am of details. You can sigh, shake your head and say *'it's more complex than that'*. But I am not required to acquaint myself with every particular before drawing general conclusions. I am not required to defend the character of every idiot who might partially agree with me. Nor am I required to demonstrate the perfection of some other set of ideas prior to criticising Islam. I may be wrong in some particulars, but I am right in general, and I don't have to be perfectly right to observe patterns. Anyone who says otherwise is a huckster seeking to advance horror behind technicalities. The evidence I advance to support my argument is every Islamic state that has ever existed in history. Disprove that.

If you don't like this book then the obligation is not on me to shut up, but on you to produce a counter argument. Explain why so much war, pollution, censorship and persecution of women and gays, and cruelty to animals is nothing to do with Islam, list the multitude of progressive Islamic societies, refresh my memory about all it's great social advances. Fill your boots!

34 – Catch 22

The more I am attacked, the more I am vindicated. To prove me wrong say I am entitled to my opinion, before calmly and thoughtfully pointing out errors.

35 – Immigrants Saved My Life

Again I don't want to bog things down with caveats but I am obliged to acknowledge there are some genuinely odious right-wing scumbags who hate Muslims just because they are different. I cannot selectively condemn the Far-Right just when it advances Islam. To clarify: The 'I' in the title of this book stands for 'Islam' not 'immigration'. I have no interest in writing an anti-immigration book, so I am drawing a distinction between the two: I disagree with Islam generally and with immigration only locally, when it is Islamic. Obviously I have to bog things down with these qualifications as mischievous people will seek to discredit my (valid) arguments with unfalsifiable accusations of thought crimes (that's what believers do).

36 – The Far-Right Want Immigration

Additionally, it's worth noting that there are various perfectly valid left-wing arguments for controlling immigration. In order to consolidate their power grab conservatives repeat the mantra that "*the far right are against immigration*". But when we attend to the empirical evidence we find (again) it's the other way round. The Right are absolutely in *favour* of immigration. Laissez faire markets are primarily about free movement. The super-rich decamp en masse to Dubai to dodge taxes, neo-capitalists constantly campaign to import low pay workers to drive down wages, and the number one motivation for migration is – money!

For the first time in history Humanity has become 'hyper-transient' meaning, large numbers of people can move large distances quickly and cheaply. This has been a catastrophe for the Left who traditionally want to plan, housing, education and health provision, which can't be done when there are large fluctuations in population. Additionally hyper-transience destabilises cultures, spreads diseases, breaks the connection indigenous cultures have with their local geography, and of course there is the pollution of the travel.

But let's set all that to one side, after all our concern here is not immigration in general but Islam in particular. Islam is a genuinely far-right ideology by every measure, those of us who oppose it do so precisely *because* we are left wing (we are in favour of women's rights, free speech, gay rights, animal rights, democracy etc). "*The far right are against immigration*" is a cynical misnomer used to demonise those who dare to speak out – it is a *genuinely* right-wing hate attack on those wishing to live in a peaceful world.

37 – The Religion IS the Problem

Every atrocity seems to follow the same pattern. Our 'leaders' automatically leap to the defence of our assailants. Information is supressed and we are told we should reserve judgement while the authorities do their job. But if the authorities were doing their job the killings would not be happening in the first place! We are eventually told that, yes, it was Islam, but the protagonists had mental health issues.

The mental illness and the religion are the same thing.
The war and the religion are the same thing.
The migration crisis and the religion are the same thing.
The population crisis and the religion are the same thing.
The 'housing crisis' and the religion are the same thing.

It wouldn't be entirely fair to say the environmental crisis and the religion are the same thing, but it wouldn't be entirely unfair either. When an ideology generates overpopulation, war, tyranny, migration and censorship, that is bound to damage the ecosystem.

When we look at the legacy media, like newspapers, it is obvious why they are dying out – when they failed to report the biggest story in the world they *chose* irrelevance.

38 – What Would I Do if I Were a Bad Person?

If I had ASPD (antisocial personality disorder) it would be convenient to convert to Islam. Every act of cruelty could be claimed to somehow advance submission. Pitiless in attack, self-pitying in defence, I would selectively appeal to human rights only when it was in the interest of myself (or my allies) to do so. Inconvenient human rights would be dismissed as incompatible with my faith. My arguments would be belief-based and therefore impervious to empirical refutation. I would masquerade as my antithesis, claiming that anyone who dissents was racist (or some other thought crime du jour) thus I could present myself as a moral hero even as I advanced submission. Every mannerism would be a microcosm of the general power grab. To prevent inconvenient questions I would say my doctrine was the final word, and that disagreement was some sinful lapse of faith. Would I be embarrassed to make extravagant claims on the basis of zero evidence? Not at all! I would call it something oxymoronic like 'true faith' and assert that virtue was directly proportional to credulity. If I wanted to shag around, I would convert to a religion designed by someone with many wives. If I wanted to abuse children, I would convert to a religion designed by someone who married an eight-year-old. If I were power crazy, I would convert to a religion designed by a dictator. And so on. It's hard to imagine an ideology more likely to punish the good and reward the bad.

Similarly, if I wanted to insult Muslims, I would say that what is good about them comes, not from their inherent human decency, but from the Koran; and that without it they would cease to be proper moral beings.

39 – To Do

1, House *our* homeless.
2, Deregulate *our* culture. Every week more of our pubs and clubs are closed by regulators. We need *more* pubs and live music venues so social life may flourish again.
3, Regulate *their* culture. To ensure public safety most operations are licensed, require professional indemnity insurance and must comply with regulations that become incrementally more onerous. If people are hurt because the bosses are negligent, or make false/misleading claims, the victims can claim for damages. Why is this not applied to the part of society that makes the most wars and misleading claims? Football clubs must make huge contributions to policing costs, why shouldn't mosques? Bollards are being installed around our public spaces to prevent vehicles being driven into crowds; why should the rest of us have to pay for that?
4, All international agreements merely advisory pending endorsement by referendum.
5, Import those we need, export those we don't. If you are not sure who is who, ask the voters - they'll set you straight.
6, Prosecute abusers who seek to advance submission.
7, Stop burning fuel.
8, Travel/transport less.
9, Raise well educated children.
10, Prohibit further destruction of our countryside.

Basically drink, think, debate, vote, socialise, garden, shag and love your kids. This is the first problem we can solve by having fun. I should have called this book 'Have Fun'.

40 – Thought Experiment

As a flight of fancy let's ask the mischievous question - What would happen if tomorrow every Muslim became an atheist?

For a start the vast majority of wars would de-escalate as the incessant craving to make more territory more Islamic would dissipate. Women would be better educated, consequently they would have fewer children, there would no longer be any reason to mutilate their genitals so they would have better sex. Fewer animals would die painful and terrifying deaths. Artists and intellectuals in the Islamic world would be able to pursue their learning wherever it took them without having to fear the condemnation of clerics. Former Islamic economies would no longer simply be about transporting people and minerals to and from one another. Former Muslims would earn their money monetising their minds. So carbon emissions would fall.

Would former Islamic societies degenerate into cesspits of immorality? Of course not, because the overwhelming majority of Muslims are inherently decent and moral. In fact, their societies would probably become less cruel because Islam confers absolute power which corrupts absolutely. Would the lives of former Muslims be less meaningful? No. They would still live, fall in love and die, discuss things, meet friends, and they would still marvel at the wonders of nature as humans everywhere have always done.

There can be no question the world would be a lot better off without Islam.

41 – Grounds For Optimism

Pessimism is useless, optimism is useful, so let us be optimists. At the beginning of the 19th Century, Goethe despaired "*I thank God that I am not young in so thoroughly finished a world*" but was the world finished? No. In 1919 Europe lay devastated by war and influenza. Were we finished? No. Are you more fearful of Islam than your grandparents were of Hitler's all-conquering war machine? No. Would you swap these times for those? No. Today you have access to better information, healthcare, and home comforts than those enjoyed by J.D Rockefeller (then the richest man in the world) a century ago. So why the despair? This generation is fortunate to be confronted by such a defeatable, second rate, ideology.

It was observed that there was a link between smoking and lung cancer, smoking was banned and cancer declined. Simple. It was observed that seat belts made cars safer, they were made mandatory and road deaths declined. Simple. In the late 80s it was observed that CFCs used in fridges and packaging were causing a hole in the ozone layer over Antarctica. Across the world CFCs were prohibited. The Ozone hole is now closed. We fixed it because we had to.

We seem to be legislating against every public menace except the one that makes the most war! To save the world from being engulfed in Islamic war all we need to do is politely but firmly make clear to Muslims that Islam is a problem to be legislated out of existence like any other social ill. To be pessimistic is to take a dim view of humanity and assume that better ideas never win. I think most Muslims are reasonable, decent and persuadable, if I'm wrong then all the more reason to act!

1, Half the world's population live in China and India, countries that do not share the West's delusions about Islam. So that's half the problem solved.

2, One hundred years ago there were about 100 countries. Today there are about 200 countries. There seems to be an inexorable trend for countries to become greater in number and smaller in size. Why? Because people want more control over their societies, they want government closer. This seems perfectly rational as smaller countries have higher incomes (per head of population) than the larger countries. When more people have more control over more power they have more prosperity. Islam is not about people power, it is about submission (powerlessness) and people power seems unstoppable.

3, Feminism, gay rights, democracy and free speech are ideas whose time has come, it is fanciful to suppose that clerics can resist them in the age of the internet.

4, All technological developments suggest that we are switching to renewable energy and cerebral jobs, so if the Islamic world wants to carry on selling fuel and censoring knowledge then enjoy staying poor.

5, Islamic economies only make money by transporting people and minerals to and from each other. But in the internet age there is no reason for this to happen anymore. They no longer have anything we need.

Never in the field of human conflict can so much be won so easily. Islam is a house of cards. Its collapse will be the event of our lifetimes.

42 - Conclusion

It's hard to do anything well, but I have to say this has been the easiest book I have ever written. I am also writing a book about furniture but I jumped onto finishing this as designing furniture is hard and I knew this book would be simple to crash out. I just finished it in couple of train journeys. Demolishing Islam as an intellectual system is pretty easy, the patterns are clear, their causes fairly obvious, and the counterarguments not taxing. I haven't over-elaborated with notes and references as the subject matter doesn't merit it.

Islam generates much that is bad and little that is good, and we would be much better off without it (Muslims especially). It is an intellectual desert, a blight on the world, it's every act is about the domination of territory. It is a social, ecological, and environmental catastrophe, a generator of war and inequality, a torturer of animals, a mutilator of women, a persecutor of gays and an incubator of tyranny. It offers nothing but endless conflict. It's hard to imagine anyone less qualified to pen an ethics document that Muhammad, his '*Allah*' rivals Jehovah as the most deplorable character in fiction. The foundational tenets are obvious lies. Islam fails wherever it goes. Every Islamic state that has ever existed bears witness to its shortcomings. The astonishing thing is that Islam is getting a free pass from useful idiots masquerading as moral heroes.

All goodness that comes from the Islamic world comes from the fundamental goodness of the Muslims themselves, not from any merits of Islamic ideology. What I love about the Islamic world is what I love about humans generally. What's bad about the Islamic world can be traced to the Koran specifically.

Throughout this book I have targeted the idea rather than the person. I don't want anyone to use this book as an excuse to hate people. Don't hate the person disagree with the idea. Every argument against this book will be the opposite - an attack on me, by an interested party, seeking to achieve the maximum submission of the maximum number of people. I'm a disinterested party, I'm not writing for money, fame, or notoriety; so why have I risked my life writing this? Because I want to use the limited time I have to achieve the maximum good (minimum pain) for the maximum number.

K-

Printed in Great Britain
by Amazon